Outside Lies Magic

Outside Lies Magic

Regaining History
and Awareness in
Everyday Places

John R. Stilgoe

WALKER AND COMPANY
NEW YORK

First published in the United States of America in 1998
by Walker Publishing Company, Inc.

Published simultaneously in Canada by
Thomas Allen & Son Canada, Limited, Markham, Ontario

Library of Congress Cataloging-in-Publication Data
Stilgoe, John R., 1949–
Outside lies magic: regaining history and awareness in everyday
places/John R. Stilgoe.
p. cm.
ISBN 0-8027-1340-8
1. United States—Description and travel—Psychological aspects.
2. United States—History, Local—Philosophy.   3. Walking—United
States—Philosophy.   4. Cycling—United States—Philosophy.
I. Title.
E169.04.S834   1998
973'.01—dc21   98-3790
CIP

Book design by Ralph L. Fowler

Printed in the United States of America

2   4   6   8   10   9   7   5   3   1

For

Nathaniel and Adam

Contents

Acknowledgments

MANY PEOPLE HELPED with the exploring behind this book. I thank Thomas Armstrong, Robert Belyea, Gerard Buckley, Neil Connolly, James Fitzgerald, John Fox, Henry Goldman, Amanda Keidan, Thomas Lembong, Eleanor Norris, Barney Schauble, Catherine Steindler, and Harold Tuttle. My editor, George Gibson, deserves special thanks for his encouragement and insight. And as always I thank my sons, Adam and Nathaniel, and above all my wife, Debra, whose unfailing support and energy make even the steepest hills fun.

Outside Lies Magic

One

Beginnings

GET OUT NOW. Not just outside, but beyond the trap of the programmed electronic age so gently closing around so many people at the end of our century. Go outside, move deliberately, then relax, slow down, look around. Do not jog. Do not run. Forget about blood pressure and arthritis, cardiovascular rejuvenation and weight reduction. Instead pay attention to everything that abuts the rural road, the city street, the suburban boulevard. Walk. Stroll. Saunter. Ride a bike, and coast along a lot. Explore.

Abandon, even momentarily, the sleek modern technology that consumes so much time and money now, and seek out the resting place of a technology almost forgotten. Go outside and walk a bit, long enough to forget programming, long enough to take in and record new surroundings.

Flex the mind, a little at first, then a lot. Savor something special. Enjoy the best-kept secret around—the ordinary, everyday landscape that rewards any explorer, that touches any explorer with magic.

The whole concatenation of wild and artificial things, the natural ecosystem as modified by people over the centuries, the built environment layered over layers, the eerie mix of sounds and smells and glimpses neither natural nor crafted—all of it is free for the taking, for the taking in. Take it, take it in, take in more every weekend, every day, and quickly it becomes the theater that intrigues, relaxes, fascinates, seduces, and above all expands any mind focused on it. Outside lies utterly ordinary space open to any casual explorer willing to find the extraordinary. Outside lies unprogrammed awareness that at times becomes directed serendipity. Outside lies magic.

MORE THAN TWENTY years ago, I began teaching the art of exploration at Harvard University, and I have been at it ever since. My courses and the books I have written focus on particular subjects—the creation of a national landscape as the treasure common to all citizens, the seacoast built environment, the suburban landscape after 1820, the ways modernization reshapes traditional spaces, among others—but the real focus of all my teaching is the necessity to get out and look around, to see acutely, to notice, to make connections.

Late in the 1980s I stopped distributing schedules of lectures. On the first day of class I introduce each course, show slides that outline the subject matter, hand out a reading list and examination schedule, and speak a bit about the sequence of topics. But I refuse to provide a schedule of topics. Undergraduate and graduate students alike love schedules, love knowing the order of subjects and the satisfaction of ticking off one line after another, class after class, week after week. Confronted by a professor who explains that schedules produce a desire, sometimes an obsession, to "get through the material," they grow uneasy. They like to get through the material. They like knowing the halfway point, the near end. I assure them that examinations will occur on given dates, that the term paper is due on the day I announce on the course information sheet, but then I explain that the lack of a topic schedule encourages all of us to explore a bit, to answer questions that arise in class or office hours, to follow leads we discover while studying something else. Each of the courses, I explain patiently, really concerns exploration, and exploration happens best by accident, by letting way lead on to way, not by following a schedule down a track.

My students resist the lack of topic structure because they are the children of structured learning and structured entertainment. Over and over I explain that if they are afraid of a course on exploring, they may never have the confidence to go exploring on their own. I encourage them to take a chance, and many do. My courses range in size from ten students around a seminar table to fifty in a traditional classroom, and I get to know my students. Now, more than twenty years after teaching my first course, I find myself knowing a great number of alumni. They tell me that I teach something of enduring value, not a mass of facts and figures, but a technique that produces surprise and delight, that enlivens otherwise dull days, that frees them from the ordinariness of so much learning. Day after day their postcards and letters, and now faxes and E-mail messages, arrive and sometimes I find their discoveries—and the ways they made their discoveries—so intriguing and insightful that I begin my classes by reading a line or two, then asking my students to comment.

My students often stare at me in amazement. They ask what kind of former students I have. Are they reliable or slightly odd? One has just noticed escape hatches in the floors of inter-city buses and inquired about their relation to escape hatches in the roofs of new school buses. Another has reported a clutch of Virginia-Kentucky barns in an Idaho valley and wonders if the structures suggest a migration pattern. A third has found New York City limestone facades eroding and is trying to see if limestone erodes faster on the shady sides of streets. A fourth has noticed that playground equipment has changed rapidly in the past decade and wonders if children miss galvanized-steel jungle gyms. Another has been trying to learn why some restaurants attract men and women in certain professions and repel others, and another (from the same class years ago) has found a pattern in coffee shop location. Yet another reports that he can separate eastbound and westbound passengers at O'Hare Airport by the colors of their raincoats. I look at my students and encourage their comments, suggesting that they consider the alumni remarks in terms of safety legislation or wagon-train routing or regional differences in clothing styles. By the middle of the term, my students respond, having gotten over their fear of subjects about which little is written.

Learning to look around sparks curiosity, encourages serendipity. Amazing connections get made that way; questions are raised—and sometimes answered—that would never be otherwise. Any explorer sees things that reward not just a bit of scrutiny but a bit of thought, sometimes a lot of thought over years. Put the things in spatial context or arrange them in time, and they acquire value immediately. Moreover, even the most ordinary of things help make sense of others, even of great historical movements. Noticing dates on cast-iron storm-drain grates and fire hydrants introduces something of the shift of iron-founding from Worcester and Pittsburgh south to Chattanooga and Birmingham. The storm-drain grate and the fire hydrant are touchable, direct links with larger concepts, portals into the past of industrialization.

Exploring as I teach it depends heavily on understanding the pasts that swirl around any explorer of ordinary landscape. Unlike so many historians entranced by great political, economic, and social movements, I emphasize that the built environment is a sort of palimpsest, a document in which one layer of writing has been scraped off, and another one applied. An acute, mindful explorer who holds up the palimpsest to the light sees something of the earlier message, and a careful, confident explorer of the built environment soon sees all sorts of traces of past generations. Students with no particular interest in schoolroom history involving presidential elections, treaties, and wars often awaken to the richness of spatial or visual history, simply because objects and even landscapes from the past have shaped their lives and shape them still.

In the first two decades of the twentieth century, experts advised men to have their kitchens painted apple-green. The experts believed that apple-green quieted nervous people, and especially wives beginning to think of suffrage, of careers beyond the home. Today the explorer of color schemes finds in old houses and apartments the apple-green paint still gracing the inside of the cabinet under the kitchen sink, and the hallways of old police stations and insane asylums. But did apple-green once cover the walls of urban schoolrooms? The explorer who starts to wonder at paint schemes in apartments, houses, and schoolrooms may wonder at the pastels that cover the walls of police stations today and the bold, primary colors everywhere in public elementary schools but absent from private ones. A college student only slightly intrigued by period color schemes but awakened to the art of exploration has a subject and skill that reward countless hours spent outdoors, in cabs approaching airline terminals, and in art museums. History is on the wall, but only those willing to look up from newspaper or laptop computer glimpse it and ponder.

A lot more is on the wall, too, however, and exploring ordinary landscape sharpens the appreciation and understanding of subjects from art to physics. No longer am I surprised when my students tell me that what they learned in my courses paid immediate dividends in others. Exploring a painting independently, not as a mere follower of some art critic, reveals details and patterns critics have missed, as one of my seacoast-environment-seminar students told me when she began studying the trees in the coastal-zone paintings of Rembrandt. And exploring the context in which a physics experiment occurs, really seeing it in detail and realizing that something is happening to the measuring device as well as to the material being charged with electrons, leads to discovery that impresses the physics professor, as a student in my suburbs seminar related to me before lapsing into scientific jargon I scarcely followed. When I hear such reports, I wonder if more students would do better in elementary and high school if teachers taught more about individual exploration of subjects and less about sliding smoothly along observational ruts.

Exploration is a liberal art, because it is an art that liberates, that frees, that opens away from narrowness. And it is fun.

Ordinary exploration begins in casual indirection,

in the juiciest sort of indecision, in deliberate, then routine fits of absence of mind. Follow the sidewalk, follow the street, turn right or left as the wind and sunlight or driving rain suggest. Walk three quarters of the way around the block, then strike out on a vector, a more or less straight line toward nothing in particular, follow the downgrade or the newer pavement, head for the shadow of trees ahead, strike off toward the sound of the belfry clock, follow the scent of the bakery back door, drift downhill toward the river. Bicycle to the store, then ride down the alley toward the railroad tracks, bump across the uneven bricks by the loading dock grown up in thistle and chicory, pedal harder uphill toward the Victorian houses converted into funeral homes, make a quick circuit of the school yard, coast downhill following the sinuous curves of asphalt covering the newly laid sewer line, tail the city bus a mile or two, swoop through a multilevel parking garage, glide past the firehouse back door, slow down and catch your reflection in plate-glass windows.

Why not explore by car? Automobile exploring insulates the motorist from every sort of nuance. The car moves too fast for its driver to notice much, and when it slows, it obstructs then jams traffic. Rarely can it safely pull over to the side of the road, onto the shoulder legally intended to receive it but nowadays harboring weed-masked ditches, broken glass, nails, tangled barbed wire, smashed shopping carts. Always its engine drowns out whispers; always its windows, its air-conditioning shut out odors. Always it bulks too large to turn easily into eight-foot-wide roads left from wagon days. Even when it is equipped with four-wheel-drive, trees and gates and mud and great rocks herd it back onto pavement, onto rutted roads meandering between obstacles. But worst of all for the explorer, the car attracts notice. Exploring requires the cloak of invisibility bicyclists and walkers quickly take for granted.

Bicycling and walking offer unique entry into exploration itself. Landscape, the built environment, ordinary space that surrounds the adult explorer, is something not *meant* to be interpreted, to be read, to be understood. It is neither a museum gallery nor a television show. Unlike almost everything else to which adults turn their attention, the concatenation of natural and built form surrounding the explorer is fundamentally mysterious and often maddeningly complex. Exploring it first awakens the dormant resiliency of youth, the easy willingness to admit to making a wrong turn and going back a block, the comfortable understanding that some explorations take more than an afternoon, the certain knowledge that lots of things in the wide world just down the street make no immediate sense. But exploring not only awakens attitudes and skills made dormant by programmed education, jobs, and the hectic dash from dry cleaner to grocery store to dentist. It sharpens the skills and makes explorers realize that all the skills acquired in the probing and poking at ordinary space, everything from noticing nuances in house paint to seeing great geographical patterns from a hilltop almost no one bothers to climb, are crosstraining for dealing with the vicissitudes of life. Exploring ordinary landscape sharpens all the skills of exploration.

Explorers quickly learn that exploring means sharpening all the senses, especially sight. Seeing intently means scrutinizing, staring, narrowing the eyes, even putting one's hand across the forehead to shade the eyes in one of the oldest of human gestures. The hand over the eyes shields them from some sideways, incident light, and cupping the hands around the eyes works even better. Spruce, pine, hemlock, and other coniferous trees become suddenly greener since the eyes see their colors as saturated, free of the blanching caused by dispersed light. And since the human eye evolved to see saturated color, cupping the hands around the eye makes possible more precise scrutinizing of even distant things, for the shielded eyes pierce the light haze that afflicts most places nowadays and reveal distant slopes not so much as brownish or gray, but darker blue, and the trees blue-green. Any explorer learning to look soon discovers the astounding interplay of light, shadow, and color, a gorgeous interplay that never ceases to amaze.

Until the turn of the century, noticing the interplay of light and dark and the myriad effects of interacting color across the landscape meant engaging in the study of *chromatics*, sometimes called *gentleman's chromatics* or *ladies' chromatics* by professional artists, but often called *meteorology* by well-educated people who knew that weather included far more than rain or wind. A stunning collection of "atmospheric effects," everything from mirages to double rainbows to over-the-horizon glimpses called *looming*, figured in the education of well-to-do children lucky enough to get beyond the one-room schoolhouse and prepare themselves for analyzing art, especially painting. Meteorology, art history, and geography combined to explain the wealth of meaning implicit in phrases like "the light of Tuscany" or the heritage implicit in colors like raw umber or chartreuse. So long vanished that even historians of the visual retrieve its fragments with difficulty, education in visual acuity explains both the origins of careful tourism and the care with which many people not only designed and built houses and gardens but supported efforts to beautify cities, suburbs, and even villages. Educated people looked acutely and valued landscapes and paintings and even furniture that rewarded scrutiny.

Visual education suffered first from the burgeoning of newspapers and magazines and dime-novels, all of which deflected interest toward typeset knowledge, and from lithography and other inexpensive methods of reproducing images, especially advertisements. Around the turn of the century, the proliferation of inexpensive black and white photography, then the spread of cinema houses, further deflected interest from exploring ordinary outdoor surroundings. The 1930s introduction of color photography for amateurs and cinematographers alike skewed attention further, but by then physics professors intrigued with Einstein's theories had catapulted college students, and high school students preparing for college, across Newtonian physics, especially Newtonian optics, to a science consisting largely of equations and interminable problem sets. By 1940, the old relation of visual acuity, physics, and analysis of art lay shattered, its only schoolroom artifact being a few minutes of instruction with a glass prism, a prism making a rainbow of colors in which few students ever see indigo, let alone wonder why Newton saw the color made by a New World dye explorers found by accident. Only now and then does someone rummaging among heirlooms notice that amateurs seem to have made much better photographs a century ago, that the faded images show an eerie attention to composition and chiaroscuro, certainly an attention lacking in most contemporary snapshots and homemade videotapes. Going for a walk became progressively less interesting even to educated people in the 1930s and 1940s, simply because even educated people knew less and less about the mysteries of light, shadow, and color that cloak and accentuate ordinary landscape.

Nowadays almost no one who walks under deciduous trees notices that all the spots of sunlight on the walkway, whatever their different sizes, are the same shape. The elliptical shape indicates something to anyone who notices and then thinks for a few minutes, who explores where others walk or trudge or scurry. The elliptical shape means simply that the sun is not a point source of light, that it fills a very large part of the sky indeed.

As education in visual acuity diminished, then essentially ended except perhaps for lessons in the appreciation of art and a handful of elementary lessons in oil painting, seeing became less and less rewarding, and interpreting poetry and travel narratives written in earlier eras became progressively more difficult. Smoke, for example, entranced generations of educated men and women, simply because it exercised their eyes and their minds. Ordinary wood smoke pouring from a chimney appears blue against a dark background, such as black shingles, but brownish yellow against a light one, such as a blue or overcast sky. Smoke particles disperse blue rays more than they do red and yellow ones, and when the smoke is against a light background, the viewer sees the smoke as brownish yellow because the blue rays have been scattered in all directions into the incident white light, leaving mostly blended red and yellow rays to reach the explorer.

Nowadays the explorer walking or bicycling in ordinary landscape may more easily watch the changing colors of smoke from truck and bus exhausts than from chimneys channeling wood smoke, but the explorer willing to risk a bit of rain can still study the amazing changes wrought by a few droplets of water. Tobacco smoke immediately exhaled from the mouth appears blue or brown, but smoke held in the mouth, then blown out in smoke rings perhaps, is always white. And just as the moisture in the mouth coats the sooty black particles of tobacco smoke, so mist, fog, and rain coat diesel exhaust, making it appear white.

Visibility mattered to earlier generations of educated adults, and to children learning to see acutely, so changes in weather mattered too. Prolonged periods of still air make for poor visibility simply because vast amounts of dust sink down from upper altitudes and remain near the ground until rain or snow sinks them to the surface. Sunny, windy weather sweeps dust particles high into the atmosphere and lets explorers see miles farther than they would otherwise. Rain meant not only washed air, however, but puddles everywhere, especially in shady areas beneath trees, where explorers may venture as soon as the sun appears. Peering into one sort of puddle after another, the explorer can analyze the visual phenomena related to those made by cupping hands around eyes, learning that to look at the reflection of trees in dark puddles means seeing details in excruciating clarity. To look up at the trees means having one's fringe vision dazzled by the incident sunlight, but to look down into the puddle surrounded by dark earth means to see the reflection free of annoyance. Out for a walk after the rain means not only peering into one type of puddle after another, however, but seeing how clean air opens on all sorts of reflections.

Today explorers must teach themselves the lessons of visual acuity long absent from grammar schools and universities, and they can learn only by looking hard. Out for a walk, out for a bicycle ride, the explorer looks at a new-mowed lawn and realizes that the strips look different when viewed end-on. Where the lawn mower moved away from the explorer, the swaths look lighter in color, but where the machine moved toward the explorer, the swaths look darker. The explorer eventually realizes, having stopped and scrutinized and thought, that the swaths that appear lighter do so because they reflect more light, and they reflect more light because the grass is laid down away from the explorer. Trespassing on the new-mowed lawn offers even more to ponder. At right angles, the swaths disappear completely, but from the middle of the lawn, as the explorer turns around, the light-dark relation reverses. And having noticed the light-dark relation, the explorer meandering through an ordinary suburban landscape begins to see the patterns in American lawn mowing, the lawns mowed in concentric squares, the lawns mowed diagonally to houses, the lawns that at first seem to contradict all the lessons of gentlemen's or ladies' chromatics, those lawns where the fertilizer spreader missed whole swaths. The explorer notices and ponders and notices, and even when the explorer cannot at first account for the interplay of light and shadow and color, say the bold, rich blue of the explorer's shadow when crossing the green lawn, at least the explorer has something to think about.

THIS IS A straightforward guidebook to exploring, but not a comprehensive study of any of the things mentioned in it. It suggests that a little acute observation of ordinary things like power lines, railroad rights-of-way, post office equipment, back roads and shopping districts, alleys and the interstate highway system, fences and revitalized main streets, even motels and highway interchanges opens up larger issues that invigorate the mind, that entice understanding, that flex mental muscle, that fit the explorer for further exploring. It is a book about awareness in ordinary surroundings. It is a book about awareness that builds into mindfulness, into the enduring pleasures of noticing and thinking about what one notices.

I hope this book encourages each reader to widen his or her angle of vision, to step sideways and look at something seemingly familiar, to walk a few paces and see something utterly new.

I also hope this book makes each reader aware that his or her personal observations and encounters in the most ordinary of landscapes can and will raise questions and issues routinely avoided by programmed educational and entertainment authorities.

And I hope this book makes each reader aware that education and entertainment media teach nothing about being original, about being innovative, about being creative or inventive. How does one learn to be creative? How does one develop the ability to produce lots of new ideas, to respond to problems easily and energetically? I think the answers lie outdoors.

Exploration encourages creativity, serendipity, invention.

So read this book, then go.

Go without purpose.

Go for the going.

How to begin? As an introduction, as a straightforward guide into the art of walking or bicycling with eyes open, mind aware, body relaxed, following and noticing the skeleton framework of electric and other lines will do. After all, not long ago wise observers worried that the telegraph, telephone, and electric wires were the snare of modernism, a great net strung over the heads of the unwary, a web that snatched ideas and dreams and independence.

TWO

Lines

ELECTRIC LINES GLISTEN, especially at sunrise and sunset when the low-angled sun bounces from their high-tech metallic covering. Everywhere electric companies abandon the not-quite-waterproof black rubberized covering that protected cables since Edison's time. So even on an overcast day the explorer glances up at silvery wires, the great spider's web slung just above the national landscape.

Wood poles carry electric wires, and telephone and cable television lines too. Nothing screams more loudly of the still-developing-nation status of the United States than the creosote-treated poles, all slightly out of perpendicular, marching along almost every road as they once marched across the plains in the hoofprints of the Pony Express. Other nations, at least in cities and suburbs, preferred steel pylons from the start, or snaked their cables underground in conduits, safe from lightning strikes, snowstorms, falling tree limbs, even errant motorists, and even now in Japan, Germany, and elsewhere, rural families expect that someday overhead wires will disappear beneath road surfaces. But not so in the United States, land of cheap timber, vast distances, and an easygoing willingness to accept the poles that warp and twist and finally rot. In the 1880s the first electricity-making companies grabbed telegraph and telephone technology and lit up cities, then small towns, then suburbs, always using wood to carry the spark.

Wood poles and copper wires paralleled railroad lines beginning in the 1840s. Telegraph technology kept trains from ramming each other. From one station to the next, the dot-dash-dot clicking of the telegraph key and sounder carried orders from the dispatcher, stopping one train, advancing another, sidetracking a third. The chattering of Morse code entranced all forward-looking Americans before the Civil War, for it announced messages moving as fast as light. No longer did vital news come by stagecoach or post rider. Now it arrived in a burst of chattering chirps, from a special sounder perched on a little shelf in the bay window of the small-town depot, a sounder adjacent to one reserved for railroad-train orders, a sounder eventually owned by a consortium of short-distance companies linked under the name of Western Union. News bulletins only interrupted the ordinary flow of private messages sent from one person to another, one company to another, but sometimes they interrupted the periodic dispatches sent by "wire service" reporters to newspaper editors. By the 1880s, telegraph operators often monitored several sounders, including one dedicated to play-by-play reports of sporting events or minute-by-minute news of ballot counting. Men and women desperate for up-to-date information gathered at the railroad station, sometimes in hotel lobbies, now and then at storefront telegraph offices for news of boxing matches, horse races, steamship sinkings, commodity- and stock-market fluctuations, war.

And around noon they drifted to telegraph offices for the time signal, the announcement of precise noon that flashed across the United States once each day, the single click of the telegraph sounder that enabled bankers and shoemakers to synchronize their watches with those of railroad conductors and engineers, to see how accurately their timepieces ticked, the single click that killed rural time, small-town time, personal time.

Inventors created gadgets to change clicks into instantaneous hard copy. Typewriter technology merged with telegraph equipment to produce machines that not only sent messages along telegraph wires but received them as electric impulses and converted them to typewritten pages. Other inventors, despairing of teaching businessmen to type, created stylus-and-metal-plate gadgets that converted handwriting to electricity that simultaneously twitched pen-holding wands into duplicating—more or less— the handwriting from afar. Best known of all, ticker tape converted code into hard-copy records of stock- and commodity-market fluctuations, and the Teletype in newspaper backrooms transmitted dozens of stories that never saw newsprint. A century before the fax, telegraph wires carried millions of messages converted from paper to electricity to paper, and other millions sent from terminals to printers.

Yet always the message charged along wires supported on wood poles. By the 1880s, urban poles carried hundreds of wires each, dozens for train dispatching near great terminals and freight yards, but scores more for telegrams, the inexpensive but brusque daytime messages delivered by Western Union messengers on bicycles, the extremely cheap messages sent in the wee hours of the morning, the telegraph-company "night letter" hand-delivered after daybreak. Not until the great snowstorm of 1888 brought down thousands of poles did New York City mandate the installation of underground tunnels for telegraph and other wires, creating one of the visual signatures of *city*. Real cities have underground wires, not lines strung atop unpainted wood poles, the poles that by 1900 carried telephone lines from house to house.

While telegraph poles marched mostly along railroad tracks, telephone poles marched —and staggered —along almost every street, almost every rural road. Until the merger of most local firms into the Bell System, many residential and small-town commercial streets had poles on both sides, since some families chose one voice-message provider while neighbors chose competitors. Away from Main Street, low-voltage telephone lines stretched away from poles to run from house to house, from barn to bridge to tree to barn, from fence post to fence post, the single telephone cable sometimes slung just beneath another wire, the lightning catcher linked every few hundred feet to wires grounding it to buried copper rods. But in suburbia, every sixty feet, every ninety feet, the distance depending on the thickness of the poles and the number of cables above, sprouted rough-hewn telephone poles slathered in creosote.

And in the very first years of the new century, street trees began to die. Telephone companies pruned the crowns of trees in order to prevent ice storms from bending limbs into contact with lines and shorting them out, even breaking them. Near downtown areas, where poles carried wide cross-arms laced with cables, telephone companies pruned further and further, and in time began removing entire trees, especially those so heavily sheared that they died soon after surgery.

Electricity companies soon decimated the national urban and suburban street tree population, precipitating by 1920 a nationwide uproar. Once alternating-current electricity flowed along cables hung above the telephone lines, street trees had to be lopped far back, or even removed wholesale, lest their branches touch the cables and short-circuit the electricity directly to the ground, igniting the tree and electrocuting any bystanders.

Electricity transmission created the trolley car and its larger, swifter, rural cousin, the interurban electric car. Almost silent, extremely inexpensive to build, and operating along roadway tracks vastly less expensive to install than private right-of-way railroad tracks, the slithery electric car swept everywhere across the nation after the 1890s, drawing its power from its trolley pole gliding under a bare electric wire strung from telephone poles. Heavy wire sometimes required poles on both sides of the road, each pair holding a heavy support wire itself carrying at right angles the trolley power line snaking above the tracks. Less-traveled trolley lines made do with trolley wires suspended over track and roadway on enormous brackets jutting out under the ordinary electricity wires, but placed above the less-hazardous telephone lines. On curves especially, trolley companies erected mazes of supply, support, and pull-off wires, the whole arrangement that made up what everyone knew as *overhead electric catenary* and threw weblike shadows over dirt roads and brick streets.

Two kinds of electricity coexisted fitfully atop the poles. Telephone and trolley wires carried direct-current electricity, cheap to produce, extremely constant—*clean* in the jargon of 1900—but difficult to send over long distances. As early as the first continental telegraph line that replaced the Pony Express, electrical engineers knew about voltage drop and understood that the wire west of St. Louis would have to be as thick as a man's thigh to get the Morse code spark across the Rockies. Instead they invented recharging units that strengthened the spark. Electricity companies abandoned direct current almost at once and provided alternating electricity to businesses and homes, the harder-to-manufacture, "noisy," but cheap-to-transmit sixty-cycle-a-second kind that, by 1905, up-to-date citizens knew as *juice*. And instead of recharging units, the electricity companies installed transformers, immense cylinders placed out of harm's way atop the poles. Essentially electricity pumps, transformers simply transform electricity, either pumping it up to race farther along the line, or pumping it down every few houses to the 110-volt/220-volt standard each family uses for lighting and for high-current appliances, mostly stoves, water heaters, and clothes dryers. Telephone lines required junction boxes here and there, but transformers soon hung everywhere, the cylindrical fruit of the electric tree, the enduring memorial of a technological battle fought between Edison, Westinghouse, and other inventors who disagreed about the relative merits of direct current and alternating current.

And they hummed. Alternating current hums. People with acute hearing know when the electricity fails even if they see no lights blink off, hear no appliances stop dead. In an instant the quiet home goes silent. In the wee hours of the morning, a power failure wakes some people because the background hum ends abruptly. Members of symphony orchestras loathe the hum as the background noise they always hear, especially when reading sheet music, in what others consider silence, but few other occupational groups give it much notice. By contrast, housewives, in the first years of the century, feared that electricity leaked from any outlet lacking a plugged-in lamp, and worried that leaking, humming electricity caused headache and cancer. Long after the direct-current-powered trolley car glided past, its trolley wheel sparking just enough to leave an odor of ozone scenting the air, its eerie echo endured, the almost imperceptible humming of the adjacent wires and transformers carrying alternating current, the wires explorers still call *live*.

Live wires leak. Explorers scrutinizing a wood utility pole often find a thick copper wire leading down the pole to an even thicker copper rod pounded into the earth. The wires ground the poles and wires during lightning strikes and help keep transformers from exploding dominolike down whole streets, one after another as the immense jolt races through the system to the earth. Late in the 1880s, water-supply and gas-supply companies discovered that electricity leaking from trolley car lines followed water and gas pipes for miles toward the powerhouse dynamos. The rogue electricity, called *stray electricity* by its angry discoverers, destroyed iron and steel piping in the process researchers quickly christened *electrolysis*, and when pipes finally burst, often leaked into subterranean electric and telephone lines too. Lawsuits and legislation combined to force street railway companies to ground their wires and rails as perfectly as possible, but even now the explorer sniffing the dawn air wonders about the whiff of natural gas. Has electrolysis destroyed a gas-main connection?

Maybe. Risk-taking explorers who push against the orange plastic temporary fencing surrounding a deep hole dug in the street, who amble up to the half-fenced hole and stare down into the gloom, discover the never-mentioned reason for the cordons put around holes. No utility company wants close inspection of its unearthed hardware. The gas company especially worries about the public seeing corroded mains and pipes, and water-supply workers struggle hard to keep inquisitors from seeing rusted mains and brittle shut-off valves. But the explorer who ventures out on a hot summer afternoon, who sniffs the ozone of an approaching thunderstorm and goes for a walk, quickly sees the stunning impact of potential lightning. Construction crews quit work early, pull steel plates over the holes, get away from faulty grounds. Every time a gas-company maintenance crew cuts a gas main, its employees clamp a metal bridge to the pipe, and cut beneath the bridge, on the off chance that electrical service in some house or office or factory is grounded to a gas pipe, not a water main. Without the bridge, a spark might jump across the cut and ignite the gas. And even with it, a lightning strike can follow a gas main to its weakest point. Electricity hums and leaks and goes places no one intends.

Explorers know the electric hum. When they walk or pedal along residential streets at daybreak, only the call of birds masks it. Let the birds fall silent, and the hum comes and goes with the hum of tires on smooth pavement. But here and there the hum grows louder.

Chain-link fences capped with razor wire keep explorers away from the immense outdoor transformers that punctuate so many residential neighborhoods. Along some leafy street, surrounded by houses, sits a quarter acre of steel and copper transformers painted green or black, a dozen gray cabinets securely locked and decorated with bright yellow warning stickers, perhaps a pole or two, always one fitted with bright lights. Little substations hum louder than overhead electric lines and transformers, but do they leak electricity through the ground only or through the air as well? Now and then an explorer walks two blocks from home, stands in front of the substation, and pulls out a pocket compass. The needle flickers, swings about, often points anywhere but north, unless north lies beyond the chain-link fence.

Explorers of ordinary space carry pocket compasses to detect magnetic fields. They play the adolescent "let's find electricity" game of the first years of the century, holding the compass as they pass red-brick buildings, stand atop urban manhole covers, walk past suburban substations. Explorers discover the ubiquitous, unsigned presence of high-voltage, high-amperage electricity everywhere and remember their high school physics lesson. A well-grounded person standing below an energy source, say a bare-foot pedestrian standing atop a concrete sidewalk below a streetlight, becomes an electricity conductor exactly as an electric capacitor functions. Sometimes, if the power source is strong enough and the explorer is well enough grounded, the explorer can almost feel the charge, say when the explorer pushes onto a power line right-of-way.

At right angles to local distribution wires run the long-distance, high-tension, high-voltage electric lines, the immense cables held aloft on metal pylons or at the end of their long runs, atop the tallest of wooden poles. Motorists driving under such lines notice only a momentary crackle of their radios and don't realize that the crackle is static caused by stray electricity. Explorers know better. They hear the hum, sometimes feel the static on their skin, feel their skin hair rise as the lightning storm swings across the lines above them.

High-tension lines run along dedicated rights-of-way either owned or leased by electricity companies. The great swaths plunge through any kind of built fabric, even cities, but where property values are very high the pylons stand higher, raising the juice-filled cables a hundred feet above shopping-mall parking lots, around factories, alongside interstate highways. Elsewhere the swaths cut lower but wider through suburban neighborhoods, through forest and farmland, across parks. Nothing tall, nothing *that might fall across,* stands near the high-tension wires, and nothing more than stubby, *nothing that might reach up,* stands beneath them. While the electricity companies permit farmers to raise crops beneath the high-tension wires, while they understand that the wires might safely cross a parking lot, every few years the companies chop down trees rising along the right-of-way and even cut the brush. Nothing must grow tall enough to carry some storm-induced spark between the high-voltage line and the ground. Nothing must ground out the electricity already straining at its confining cables. Nothing must mask the inspector's gaze down the right-of-way.

Power line rights-of-way are unnoticed—perhaps *unrealized* is a better word, because only to explorers are the rights-of-way real—highways lacing the whole country, the routes intrepid and trespassing explorers follow to shortcut across country. Landowners erect signs and fences, but the explorer knows that every right-of-way includes a dirt track for maintenance vehicles, a dirt track often deliberately camouflaged where it intersects any motor vehicle road, a dirt track gated against motor vehicles but accessible to any explorer willing to look for it along the road shoulder and willing to risk trespassing a bit. The early-morning explorer trespassing along the electric right-of-way discovers how much wild animals depend on the alternate highway system, how even large species like deer move along the power company routes between wilderness and state parks and privately owned clumps of forest. Only where the rights-of-way cross a paved or dirt road do power companies let the brush and trees grow higher, partly to keep motorists from noticing the supposed ugliness of the right-of-way itself, partly to keep secret its easiest access points. But that high-growing brush often shelters raccoons and coyotes, even elk and moose and bear waiting to cross the line of cars intersecting their route, and the explorer who slows down, approaches from downwind, and looks *in* at the leafy gloom often sees the eyes watching back.

Other rights-of-way resemble the high-voltage one. Natural gas and crude-oil pipelines run across much of the South and the West and snake far into the North, always far less visible to the speeding motorist because the pipes lie buried. But trees stand cleared from them too lest roots disturb the pipes, and always a dirt track, often much less noticeable than electricity company ones because much less frequently used, runs amid the weeds. From Louisiana and Texas and Oklahoma north, east, and west run the pipeline rights-of-way, sometimes merging with the electricity rights-of-way and reaching into the most distant states, leading the explorer as secretly as any coyote deeper and deeper into the woods, across farmland, through suburbs, on and on.

Electricity rights-of-way and some pipeline rights-of-way run as rivers flow in deltas. To explore upstream means to notice diverging lines, to watch the cables grow thicker, steel pylons replace wood poles, then the pylons grow taller. Finally, miles and states away, the walking or bicycling explorer crests a hill and sees ahead the cooling towers of the power plant or the immense maze of pylons and transformers beside the hydroelectric dam or finds some refinery lit up against the night. Under the wires, surrounded by the hum, atop the throbbing gas, the explorer eats lunch or dinner, grins in satisfaction at finding a dining place impossibly remote from the imaginations of most people, at the end of a shortcut between highways, perhaps, or a route that opens on thousands of backyards and unshaded windows.

Cable television offers no such route, no such vista. Cable television companies send long-distance signals by satellite and so lack long-distance lines, but their short-distance cables cling everywhere to poles originally intended only for electricity and telephone cables. Low down on the poles, the television company cables dangle from second-thought brackets, droop from pole to pole, pole to house. Unlike its well-heeled, public utility counterparts, cable television hangs in limbo, still not recovered from wiring the nation in a decade, often unable to upgrade its network, dependent on a system of coaxial cables thicker than telephone lines and more fragile. And now its counterparts need more room on every pole.

So why not look at every pole along a short residential street, along a half mile of rural road? Why not explore by looking upward, just for a few minutes? Most people, especially those walking or running or bicycling for physical exercise, tend to look where they are going. The explorer looks ahead too, of course, but also sideways and backward, assimilating a wide field of landscape indeed. But explorers who discover so much in the 360-degree circle they scan know too how much lies downward, often almost under their feet, and they scrutinize everything from pavement types to wildflowers. And the canniest explorers look up too, up at clouds and sky and birds, up at airplanes, up at utility poles, and in looking up they descry something of the complexity of the high. They spot advertising blimps, and kites long snared in trees; they marvel at the television antennae lingering from decades ago and notice the decrepitude of so many domestic and industrial chimney tops. They see not only the changing number of cross-arms and cable types atop utility poles but the growing numbers and shapes of cables. With a bit of practice, and a bit of noticing what sort of utility line worker repairs what sorts of wires, they differentiate between neighborhoods newly rewired and streets on the margins of electrical modernization. Explorers see The Internet against the sky and watch the demand for electricity and communication services change the face of every street.

Rising demands for electricity, especially for air-conditioning in the South, and for telephone service, especially additional lines for fax machines and computer modems, prompt electricity and phone companies to upgrade services, to squabble over every pole, every route. Wood cross-arms vanish as new-style brackets carry the far thicker, metal-sheathed cables that increase electricity capacity ten times over and decrease the number of transformers, but that require taller poles and massive street-tree trimming to eliminate the greater chance of accidental grounding. But lower cross-arms carried telephone lines, and so the phone companies devise thicker, bundled cables suspended from heavy metal brackets, and here and there along the road erect green-painted switching boxes to save pole space. Everything aloft is higher up, so every "drop," every connection between pole and structure, is reangled, and more trees are trimmed, until suddenly the explorer realizes that the street trees are gone, that more cables, and thicker cables, run along the road, and that new cables begin to appear, especially the wave-of-the-future fiber-optic ones often sheathed in corrugated orange plastic.

Electricity, phone, and cable television companies alone are not responsible for the death of street trees, for the transformation of street and road vistas. Springtime explorers see another reason, at least in the North. Salting roads to melt snow and ice poisons roadside vegetation, sometimes quickly, sometimes slowly. The salt that kills maples and oaks rewards halophyte species like poison ivy, but in the end it eliminates the canopy of overhead greenery that scatters sunlight and shades pavement. Explorers sniff another killer. At dawn, they now and then get a whiff of leaking gas, know that somewhere under their feet or their spoked wheels a gas main lies ever so slightly fractured. At daybreak, when the air is still, the odor is barely discernible. An hour later, as the first breezes rise and the first unleaded-gas automobiles roll, their exhaust sometimes smelling like escaping gas and their motion roiling the air along the roads, only a rare child waiting for a school bus may smell the gas. But the gas permeating the soil chokes trees, especially mature trees struggling against the sun-heated soil beneath the asphalt, the all-night streetlight illumination, the spray of salt every winter. So the dawn-chasing explorer weaves from side to side, sniffing, looking, figuring out under which side of the pavement the gas line lies buried, evaluating the health of street trees, then looking ahead at the poles and wires no longer masked by leaves but starkly screaming the webbing.

And the explorer notices something else. Expensive new houses, expensive new subdivisions stand miles away from high-voltage electric lines. Since the late 1980s, real estate developers have known that wealthy people who can choose where to live will not live near high-voltage power lines for fear of cancer. The explorer probing carefully along the rights-of-way discovers what is not there. No rich people live in new houses near power lines, and rich people fight the routing of new electric lines, especially long-distance electric lines, anywhere near their homes. And they fight the reactivation of railroad lines too.

EVERYWHERE THROUGHOUT THE COUNTRY, the scrutinizing walker or bicyclist finds the derelict railroad rights-of-way memorializing the post-1920 victory of the automobile. Usually only the roadbed remains, an almost perfectly level embankment of gravel topped with cinders and crushed stone snaking its way through woods, across swamps, behind the backs of stores. Grown up in mature trees or still open in scrubby plants like sweet fern, the roadbed often displays a haphazard footpath, what colonial French explorers called a *trace*, a mere line of footprints. Children and teenagers make the railroad-bed footpath and thereby know the secrets of railroad making. Civil engineers laid out almost level routes shortcutting across country, because they worked not only under the difficulties of making steel wheels grab steel rails but under the orders of corporations far more powerful than any municipality or county building dirt roads. Only where the footpath intersects paved roads does it vanish behind the camouflage that deflects the attention of motorists, especially police officers reluctant to abandon patrol cars and follow the trace.

Any contemporary explorer who deserts the paved road for the roadbed footpath moves into a time tunnel. Overarched by mature trees that shade the right-of-way, bordered by dense woods and tall, thick brush, the roadbed winds unseen and unnoticed even by its abutters, forgotten by entire populations. Everything within the leafy corridor, or within the grassy corridor separating pastures and arable fields, once crackled with the highest tech of all, however, and here and there the explorer of ruins discerns the remnants of technology decayed.

At either side march the fence posts carrying the barbed wire or netlike woven wire railroad companies used to defend their property against trespass. Often the wire endures, maintained by homeowners and farmers and factory owners as a sort of decrepit boundary smothered in bittersweet and other climbing vines, but more often it lies buried in leaves, long free of the wood or metal stakes tipped drunkenly along the frontier between traditional rural or small-town or suburban landscape and railroad corridor space. The fences remind the explorer that between the two derelict fences surged something demanding defense, the iron horse that behaved unlike any creature of God. But what sort of defense? Did it need defending against errant cows, or did abutters demand to be fenced from it?

Such questions weave into a thousand others. Exploring a long-abandoned railroad route means deciphering if not exactly following a ribbon of argument. Questions and surmises and sometimes answers diminish to whispers perhaps, but sometimes explode before the explorer who realizes that as the railroad bed is now, so someday might be the high-speed highway. So well built were most railroads that everyone considered them *permanent ways*, the term by which they are legally known sometimes in Europe, often in Africa and Asia. The gentle undulation of the roadbed, the sinuosity of the curves around hills, the massive culverts carrying insignificant streams beneath the ballast—all imply an implacable, indomitable engineering. And the explorer who looks carefully, who pushes away vines from the hewn-stone blocks, who squats down and squints along the dead-level, perfectly straight roadbed streaking into the overgrown vegetation a half mile ahead, realizes that something not visible made the railroad corridor a ruin. The permanent way turned out to be impermanent indeed, but so well built that it endures without maintenance. The explorer scrutinizing a contemporary abandoned railroad corridor walks across the abyss of time so few people bridge, and confronts the everlasting solidity of Egyptian pyramids and Inca roads.

When the railroad ruled America, even small children knew it ruled by physical size and technological supremacy, not merely because its corporate owners and stockholders controlled state legislators and members of Congress. After the Civil War, the locomotives grew ever more massive, towering over anything but trees and two-story buildings, and the trains grew longer and longer, until by World War I mile-long freight trains crept along the rails, which were shared by ninety-mile-an-hour express passenger trains composed of a few Pullman cars each eighty feet in length. Long before small towns and farmhouses boasted electric light, the nighttime passenger train advertised its incandescent brightness, and while farmers heated kitchens with wood and bathed in tin tubs, Pullman passengers swept past warmed by steam heat and luxuriating in hot showers.

On cold winter nights the throaty roar of the steam whistle echoed for miles along valleys and across prairies, and the brilliant locomotive headlights stitched the countryside like so many lighted needles poking the darkness. Humid summer nights made the whistles sound almost mournful and kept the smell of coal smoke lingering long after the slow freight or air-conditioned passenger train had become only a pair of red lights twinkling miles off or a faint throbbing sound finally overwhelmed by crickets or silence.

Every freight train rolled emblazoned with boxcars labeled for places as mysterious or mundane as Bangor & Aroostook, Moscow, Camden, & St. Augustine, Illinois Central Gulf, the Milwaukee Road, and Atchison, Topeka, and Santa Fe, or they carried names less easy to find in schoolroom atlases, names like Cotton Belt, Nickel Plate Road, Old Colony, Southern Pacific, and Grand Trunk Western. Every mail train rolled like lightning, never stopping at small towns but instead flinging out a sack of first-class mail even as a pistol-packing railway post office clerk leaned from an open door and swung the hook that grabbed and pulled in the sack of mail hanging from a crane by the depot platform. Every passenger train—from the local puffing asthmatically from small town to small town to the transcontinental express roaring from city to city without pause—offered the spectacle of escape into the metropolitan corridor, into modernity.

And the lines of trains rolled in a corridor of their own. Steel rails, each forty feet long, lay spiked atop creosoted wood ties themselves set twelve inches apart atop crushed stone or cinder ballast. Beside the track marched the telegraph poles carrying the telegraph and signal wires along which train-control messages flashed, and here and there a signal mast rose to carry the red, amber, and green lights that directed engineers. Decade after decade, railroad companies improved corridor technology, sometimes shifting quickly, say from kerosene to electric lighting of signal lamps, sometimes moving reluctantly from stone-block culverts to concrete-and-steel ones.

Always the corridor exemplified the triumph of engineering over topography, darkness, especially weather, for inside the two fences trains ran on time even in snowstorms and gales, or at least passengers expected them to do so. Time outside the corridor fences might be seasonal or cyclical or vague, but along the elevated rails it ticked away as standard time, zoned time, railroad time. Paying passengers entered corridor technology and corridor time through the street doors of great urban terminals and small-town depots, but only when they boarded the milk train or the local passenger or the 5:34 commuter did they give themselves wholly to railroad technology and railroad time, depending for their safe arrival on signals looming far ahead and expecting to arrive on time no matter what.

So magnetic did the railroad prove that soon whole cities, whole counties rearranged themselves, if indeed the railroad did not precede almost everything else homesteaders built, as it did across much of the Great West. The explorer weaving along the grown-up right-of-way discerns how roads and hamlets and factories focus still on the long-gone tracks, how suburbs orient themselves toward the ballast, how on clear winter days hilltop mansions look down now on the trainless, trackless ribbon of plant-studded ballast.

Far out in the countryside of large estates and hobby farms, the bicyclist probing the right-of-way realizes that once long-distance commuter trains connected the opulent country homes with cities and great factory districts. And the walker glancing down at the ballast occasionally discerns a wider swath of cinders or a ten-foot-wide pavement of shrub-blanketed brick, and knows that where trees now stand a tiny station stood. And the bicyclist can crouch low over the handlebars, shift down and down, and probe the half-foot-wide path that leads at right angles from the brick-paved platform into the brush, uphill, suddenly onto a near-silent residential street lined with gated driveways. Or the walker emerges thoughtfully from the woods or fields and finds a tiny industrial park of grain elevators, machinery dealers, warehouses, wood-frame or redbrick factories, every structure marked by that certain sign of railroad influence, the walled-up loading doors four feet above grade level, too high for trucks but the perfect height for boxcar floors. Or the explorer walking or biking crests a hill in winter when the fallen leaves offer a wide view and sees stretched out a sinuous redbrick industrial landscape now crosshatched by paved roads but definitely following its long-gone armature of steel rails.

What too many educated Americans dismiss as

suburban sprawl if they pause to consider it at all, what makes no immediate sense to the motorists driving post–World War II highways, the discovering, almost bushwhacking explorer immersed in corridor shadows realizes as impeccable landscape order now cluttered, indeed obscured with modern junk.

Now and then stepping gingerly over a few creo-soted ties somehow left behind to rot imperceptibly over the decades, once in a while rolling over a massive, permanent culvert standing strong against spring freshets, more rarely seeing the poison-ivy-covered signal mast staring eyeless into the woods behind, the contemporary explorer strains to see ahead through the brush, into the past. Bridges remain as well, sometimes wood trestles secure in creosote and so isolated that no arson-minded vandals know of them, and here and there an interlocking tower, the blocky, two-story building that contained the foolproof signaling mechanisms railroad companies installed at junctions to prevent train collisions. At immense intervals the explorer finds a water tower or water plug, whose spout locomotive crews jerked down in a brief operation that produced the term *jerkwater town* for hamlets lacking any other reason for a train to stop.

Rusted and toppled, broken windowed and half burned, always dilapidated but somehow enduring in its nineteenth-century built-forever corporate capitalist way, the abandoned railroad corridor rewards any explorer at all intrigued by industrial archaeology, linear ecology, historical geography, and it rewards any explorer anxious to shortcut well-used highways, to probe the gently graded routes around which the contemporary built environment still nestles.

And so sometimes the explorer emerges from cinders and sumac into a parking lot, perhaps, and finds ahead the roadbed groomed and even asphalt paved, made into a bicycle path by "rails to trails" folks anxious to get bicyclists, especially young bicyclists, off busy streets, and to provide smooth walking for the elderly and for parents pushing strollers. And at first the four-foot-wide bike path strikes the bicyclist explorer as really rather pleasant, easy to ride, demanding no careful attention, presenting no dangerous interruptions. The bicyclist leans over the handlebars and begins churning, cranking faster and faster, flashing around the first gentle curve, sprinting along the tangent, leaning into another curve, thinking of the Tour de France, then surprising three young mothers with four children on tricycles and two more in strollers. The children scatter. The cyclist brakes, chooses the brush, crashes down the old railroad embankment. Above, the mothers berate. Bike paths are not for speed but for enjoyment, for the very young, the strolling old, they shout.

For the serious bicyclist, for the tandem-bicycle riders cruising at fifty miles an hour, bike paths produce trouble, filled with slow-moving obstacles, training-wheel bikes, half-balanced bicyclists, bemused bird-watchers, headphone-wearing teenagers oblivious to the silent machine racing up behind. So the federal government issues guidelines now. Wherever federal money builds a bike path—or *bikeway* as some documents now phrase it—there the pavement will be eight feet wide, with open shoulders, and even secure fences, an accommodation to the bicycle era bureaucrats foresee already this side of the horizon.

But the explorer brushing past the sumac and chokecherry trees now and then emerges into brighter daylight and spies ahead the cast-iron four-legged bumper or the pile of gravel or tossed railroad ties, which marks the end of active track. Sunshine pours in among the trees pruned away from the precious rails, and usually a switchstand signal or two mark the run-around track that permits locomotives to change ends of trains. Where the railroad ends rewards attention in the last days of the twentieth century. The explorer emerging from the past finds the weeds kept more or less at bay, perhaps by burning, perhaps by herbicide, and finds the steel rails gleaming dully in the sun. Nothing particularly high-tech reveals itself immediately, but nothing much of dereliction either. Often a track or two lies abandoned, sometimes with sapling trees grown up between the ties, and usually the telegraph poles stand bereft of wires. But grease glistens on the movable parts of the switchpoints, and bits of steel cable welded between the rail joints set the explorer to thinking. An aluminum-painted or stainless steel electrical box stands near the tracks, heavy cables snaking from it to the rails, and perhaps away to the nearest electric line. The empty freight cars standing on the spur track dwarf eighteen-wheel trucks, and beneath the names of long-merged railroad companies carry bar-code signs like those on supermarket items. The end of the line drowses in the autumn sun while the explorer stretches, then eats lunch. End of the line or head of the track?

Here between past and future, in the present of warm sunlight lingering from summer, swatting away the yellowjacket investigating the precious can of Coca-Cola just pulled from its insulating pack and opened to quench a thirst as strong as any the soft drink quenched in the 1880s heyday of the railroad, looking around with casual but deliberate awareness while unwrapping the sandwich or opening the sprouts, sitting in utterly ordinary, utterly out-of-the-way space routinely traversed only by ranging dogs, the explorer realizes again the necessity to explore, the rewards of exploring, the whole magic meaning of personal discovery.

THE EXPLORER GLANCES away from the rails curving past the old warehouse, the half-empty factory, vanishing past the long-demolished station and water tank. The explorer glances back toward the woods, the right-of-way marked only by the trace of footprints and bicycle tires. And the explorer sees the flash of fluorescent orange, sets down lunch and walks to the surveyor stake driven into the ragweed-covered cinders, reads the numbers inked on its side, sees another a hundred yards nearer the woods, and wonders about something considered, something planned, something not yet in the newspapers. After lunch the explorer walks very indirectly, counting stakes, roughly measuring paces back to the old main track, the still slightly elevated track railroaders called "the high iron." In the midst of weeds and abandonment, the explorer studies the alignment of stakes.

Anyone who explores abandoned railroad routes discerns among the nineteenth-century ruins the first indications of the next railroad age. Only railroad executives and real estate speculators, and sometimes razor-sharp state and county planners, know what computer simulations indicated as early as the 1980s, when energy-crisis-era research begun a decade earlier began to coalesce into a vision of metropolitan areas no longer dependent on private automobiles but remarkably like many in Europe and Asia. In the first years of federal deregulation, when the first massive tremors shook the trucking industry, railroad executives began rediscovering the profitability of carrying passengers. Railroad routes are valuable not only to animals wandering from woods to swamps to woods and to a handful of explorers walking or bicycling along them, but to railroad companies and public transit authorities. They know that long before the first passenger boards the first train running on restored rails, savvy real estate speculators will have made fortunes, the prospect of which sways the votes of politicians asked to restore railroad service.

Everyone exploring abandoned rights-of-way within fifty miles of any city considered major in 1920 rides in commuter country, in the borderlands of suburb and countryside. Sometimes the walker or bicyclist sees the granite or concrete mile marker left behind at railroad abandonment, and instantly realizes that the nearest urban downtown is far nearer *by rail* than by state or interstate highway. Sometimes the walker or bicyclist pauses to adjust shoelaces or toe clips or brake cables, and looks up suddenly aware that the railroad distance is a distance without traffic jams, with a guaranteed schedule between depot and terminal. So the walker moves past some local historical society building or past some grim-visaged nineteenth-century public library, then turns around and enters to find some commuter-train time-table from 1932 or 1956. Fingers running down the columns listing departure times and miles and names of stations, the explorer does a quick mental calcula-tion or two and appreciates seventy-mile-an-hour ser-vice along a shorter route than any contemporary highway. And next Saturday the explorer walks or pedals farther and farther down the abandoned right-of-way, detouring around the missing bridge, wonder-ing about long-demolished stations and the one con-verted into a liquor store, pushing toward the city and finding cities along the route.

Ordinary exploration, probing around common-place areas with nothing special to guide the mind, now and then leads the explorer into libraries and archives and gasoline stations and hairstyling salons and other repositories of information that shape the rest of the walk or bike ride. Now and then the ex-plorer discovers the quiet pleasure of using informa-tion sources not at the outset, not as some AAA Triptik to guide the whole trip, but as the prizes in some ongoing scavenger hunt.

The explorer probing metropolitan railroad rights-of-way sees around the curve of time to the biggest transformation of the United States built environment since the suburbanization that followed the interstate highway building of the 1950s and 1960s. The abandoned rights-of-way will certainly carry passengers from the farthest suburbs, the borderlands or exurbs or whatever their designation, *toward* the cities in which commuter trains terminated in the 1920s, but most passengers will leave the morning train in the satellite cities that now ring most large, older cities, the satellite cities in which so many office parks appeared in the 1970s. Only several decades ago at the edge of urban traffic jams but now extremely jammed themselves, the satellite cities offer land values substantially lower than those of central cities. They also offer nascent public-transit systems, usually bus-based systems, easily shaped and reshaped (unlike subways) to access existing and planned office parks. Often the explorer finds the right-of-way approaching satellite cities to be an active freight railroad, or at least so blocked by fences and parking lots as to be nearly impassable, even on a Sunday morning when trespass proves easiest. And the explorer turning away from it to prowl parallel streets and alleys realizes what so many motorists—and so many writers about the future of great cities—

simply miss. White-collar jobs still cluster around long-vanished railroad stations, but now long-vanished stations in satellite cities, not the long-gone terminals in once-great downtowns.

Where will they park, these railroad commuters of the immediate future? The explorer knows, for the explorer probing the rights-of-way far out from the satellite cities knows that small-town and suburban depots had very few parking spaces in the 1930s, simply because men expected to walk to stations or have their wives drop them off and pick them up. And now wives commute to work too. So tiny parking lots wreathed around charming hamlet and suburb-village depots cannot begin to accommodate the motorists arriving to board the two-story passenger trains of the future. The lots—and the stations—must be away from the old way-station commercial clusters. The lots and stations must stand where the explorer finds derelict industrial buildings or wooded land long abandoned, sites near highway access, sites showing the brush cutting of surveyors if not orange-painted stakes, sites sometimes bounded by the holes left from stakes pulled up by careful real estate developers who know how easily fluorescent orange grabs the eye of explorers focused on birds or blueberries.

Where the new lots and stations go will determine the siting of the new commercial loci, the hubs of short-distance bus lines perhaps, but certainly the sites of grocery stores, drugstores, dry cleaners, coffee shops, minimalls. And already deep-pocket real estate investors buy the sites, the places motorists never see, the places computer simulations find only after crunching census statistics, driving times, and highway routes into a stew of 1920s railroad schedule information. And already some people move away from the nodes-to-come, the transportation hubs of the next decades.

Already a handful of specialists know as certain what most Americans dismiss as daydream but the explorer knows as potential: The railroad will come again, and it will retrace its tracks. And just as real estate developers will not build expensive houses within a mile or so of high-voltage electric transmission towers, so they now avoid buying or building new homes near abandoned railroad rights-of-way, even rights-of-way more than a mile distant. They know the future of railroading is an electric-powered one dependent on overhead catenary like that stretching along the Amtrak main line between Washington, D.C., and New Haven, Connecticut, and about to extend to Boston, like that planned to cross much of Utah over Union Pacific tracks.

Catenary changes everything about living near a track. To be sure, electric locomotives are near silent, but the electric-powered trains run far faster and may well produce more vibration. Moreover, electric-powered trains stop and start more quickly, and so can be scheduled more frequently. Catenary demands a wide swath be cut along the track, for it and the rails must be protected against falling tree limbs. Catenary transmission poles rise above treetops, so that the railroad route is not lost in the greenery that camouflages most abandoned rights-of-way, but is obtrusive indeed even in long-distance, down-the-valley views. Catenary carries the high-voltage electricity that worries so many health-conscious people, including those wealthy enough to move far from it. But more than anything else, catenary-supported passenger railroads attract everything human to the railroad corridor, bringing not only increased commercial development but increased highway traffic, then demands for zoning changes. And as some real estate developers avoid any disused railroad corridor no matter how overgrown, other speculators arrive to invest in the next land boom.

Paused for a moment, looking around with a bit more care than usual, the explorer realizes that long ago people, baggage, freight, and the mail traveled together and stopped at the same stations. How fast did a letter move in the days when dozens of trains swept along main line tracks, when clerks sorted the mail in every car of the railway post office? Has the mail slowed down since steam locomotive days? Did the Post Office once offer same-day delivery of ordinary letters? What is a public highway if not the way of the letter carrier? The explorer pauses, sees the mailbox sited by the side of the road, not the track, and wonders who knows the answers.

Three

Mail

ONCE THE POST Office knew public from private space. Not long ago, a public way welcomed a letter carrier, either a carrier walking from house to house, leather bag slung over shoulder, or, after the turn of the century, a rural carrier offering the new rural free delivery (RFD) to every farmer who had erected a metal box atop a post. Always country folk endured a different standard than city people, however. Anywhere the urban or town letter carrier strode, the mail strode in majesty from sidewalk onto front walk, up front stairs, across porch boards to the mailbox screwed beside front doors. The letter carrier risked all sorts of dangers on the public sidewalk, but once onto private property the letter carrier risked tripping over abandoned roller skates, stumbling over toy soldiers, and above all, being attacked by errant watch-dogs defending home turf. No one doubted the privacy of the property within the hedge or picket fence, but no one doubted the right of postal workers to stride or amble up the walk, hands filled with first-class mail, eyes shifting between addresses and lurk-ing dogs. But away from city sidewalks, people ex-pected something different.

At first, they expected almost nothing. Until the turn of the century, rural Americans had to visit post offices to pick up their mail and to send letters, and even then the Post Office handled no packages. For decades, political patronage determined which store-keeper acted as postmaster: The shifting fortunes of Federalists and Whigs, then Democrats and Republi-cans, shifted the stamps, cash drawer, and pigeon-holes from one general store to another. Making the Post Office less political at first made little differ-ence, since storekeepers often bid on the right to sell stamps and postmark letters, seeing the postal busi-ness as attracting customers interested in more profitable items like crackers. Only cities and large towns boasted freestanding post offices dedicated solely to postal operations. Small towns and cross-roads hamlets knew only the partitioned-off sections of general stores, each with a counter crowded on Saturdays. Then in the first years of the twentieth century came rural free delivery and its companion service, parcel post.

But neither service brought mail carriers down the long lanes that ended in farmyards. Instead rural carriers left letters, newspapers, and eventually the packages that enriched Sears and Roebuck, James Cash Penney, and Montgomery Ward in the curve-topped metal boxes they visited each day along the roadside. To be sure, RFD offered services unknown to city dwellers. Farm families could buy stamps from RFD carriers and leave letters unstamped, expecting a bill the next day. But unless they lived within a half mile of the post office, farm families expected special-delivery letters to be delivered along with ordinary mail, often a day after their receipt at the post office. Certified and registered letters might be delivered into the barnyard by a letter carrier anxious for ice water and apple pie, but sometimes produced only a slip of paper in the metal box advising a visit to the post office. And packages often meant trouble. While city residents knew parcel post traveled separately from the walking letter carrier but also arrived on the front porch, rural families knew that the boxes traveled alongside letters but often stood soaking wet against the post holding aloft the metal container too small for even a shoe box. And until World War II, when wartime shortages ended the service, city dwellers got two deliveries of mail each day. Far out in the country, farm families got only one, and it was often much delayed by stormy weather. More than anything else, postal service screamed of spatial discrimination. But always the price of the stamp remained the same everywhere in the country.

Explorers know the Postal Service as the provider of street furniture. Urban streets stand interrupted by full-size letter boxes, often two or three in a row, one each for stamped, metered, and Express Mail, and by dark green storage boxes filled and emptied once or twice each day by drivers bringing mail to walking carriers. When the explorer wanders onto older suburban streets, he or she spies the old-style pillar box, the envelope-only little boxes usually placed securely atop a concrete pillar. And farther out, all the boxes disappear and the millions of RFD boxes begin, usually along roads lacking sidewalks, but sometimes sprouting in the grassy berm between sidewalk and street. Thereafter, the scrutinizing explorer knows, deposit mailboxes appear only in front of post offices and very rarely in front of shopping plaza and shopping mall stores.

Sometimes the bicyclist explorer plays tag with the RFD carrier out ahead, the mail now and then overtaking the bicyclist, then being overtaken itself at a clutch of rural letter boxes. Any bicyclist who scrutinizes letter carriers in suburbs and small towns glimpses the power and majesty of the mail, even if in rural and wilderness regions the mail rides in a much-dented sedan driven by a plainclothes carrier. Once in a while the bicyclist sees that some houses get a bright red bulk-mail leaflet or large chartreuse envelope while others do not, or that some farmhouses receive a free sample box of laundry detergent and others get nothing but letters. No letter-carrier favoritism explains the differences, only marketing analysis.

Although a favorite target of stand-up comedians and cut-the-budget politicians, the Postal Service endures as immensely powerful, almost almighty. It carved the country into zip codes, and advertisers now target would-be customers by zip code, and even by the mail routes designated by nine-digit zip codes. Moreover, as the bicyclist learns while chatting with the RFD carrier lunching under a cottonwood tree, market-research firms now mail one sort of coupon or free sample to all the odd-numbered residences along a mail route, and another to all the even-numbered ones, then study the patterns of redemption. Every time a consumer fills out the warranty card accompanying a new camera or stove, every time a consumer subscribes to a magazine or uses a credit card, another fragment of information drops into computers running software structured by the nine-digit zip code. The Postal Service, in the slang of gangsters, knows where you live.

And never do people challenge the vast inequality of postal service. The main New York City post office stands open twenty-four hours a day, but in the hill towns of northern New Mexico, post offices open for a half hour each morning and a half hour late each afternoon. A first-class stamp buys high-speed service between Boston and Houston, Atlanta and Chicago, but far slower service between Grapevine in Arkansas and Alexander in Maine, let alone between Lost Cabin in Wyoming and anywhere. In metropolitan areas, any parcel post user can scrawl a large red star or asterisk next to the address, and the Postal Service will deliver the package the next day at no extra charge even though it rarely advertises red star delivery and few customers know to ask for it. In rural areas, even Express Mail is not guaranteed to make it to a distant city overnight, or to another RFD address in two days. But so inured are they to spatial inequality, spatial discrimination, that rural Americans rarely consider their ineligibility for special-delivery service important enough to put "RFD" on their letterheads, warning all correspondents that special delivery is not for them. Rural Americans think no one uses special delivery in these turn-of-the-century times, because, after all, special delivery never comes to them.

Nonetheless, every urban letter box gleaming in enamel paint, every RFD box standing askew in a sea of chicory and wild morning glories, stands watched over by the postal inspectors. The mail rides still as it did in the years just after Independence, when Congress knew that the only regular contact Americans had with their new government was the post office, when every post office blossomed with the federal flag and the words *United States*. After all, muses the explorer swinging past, whose post office would it be?

Suburban explorers discover mysteries in the location of drop-off boxes, even in the drop-off boxes themselves. Who decides which shopping plaza or what intersection gets a drop-off box? Who determines which boxes get morning pickups and which are emptied only late in the afternoon? Some patterns become evident to the bicyclist wheeling up to box after box, pulling down the door to read the pickup information posted inside, leaning against the box in ninety-degree heat and gulping tepid water from a plastic bottle. Lately Saturday and Sunday pickups are few, if any, and weekday-morning pickups seem more rare every year. The coming of Express Mail changed morning pickups in metropolitan areas, for the Postal Service discovered to its chagrin that flying first-class mail occasionally resulted in next-day service: An ordinary letter mailed early in the morning in San Francisco, for example, might arrive the next day in Los Angeles, even in Seattle. Wise customers would never pay for express service if first-class service worked so well, and gradually the early-morning metropolitan pickups, especially the crack-of-dawn pickups intended to reward late-night mailers, ended without obituary.

Now and then the explorer glimpses the efficiency of the past, seeing in cities and villages the post offices snuggled against the railroad tracks, and remembers that long ago the Post Office ran an immense fleet of railway post offices (RPOs) attached to passenger trains, speeding post offices that not only made possible *same-day* delivery of first-class mail between large cities like Boston and New York, but also subsidized the passengers riding in the coaches and sleeping cars behind. When the Post Office decided to fly all first-class mail, the country lost most of its inter-city passenger-train service—and its same-day, high-speed, center-city to center-city mail service too. It lost the trains that carried canoes and bicycles free in the baggage cars that rode in front of the railway post offices; the trains that linked suburbs to cities, small towns to hamlets, cities to hunting camps; the trains that made mail and baggage and cheap travel part of a larger system.

Any explorer chasing the long-canceled stamps of

long-ago Post Office routes, especially long-vanished RPO routes, sooner or later confronts the shiny boxes of the privately owned express companies like United Parcel Service, Federal Express, DHL, and the others, always ranged on private property, in front of so-called mail-box stores on Main Street, more often in front of we package-it-for-you stores along commercial strips far away from downtown. The explorer knows the end-of-day automobile traffic around the drop-off boxes, the frenzied secretaries and small-business CEOs roaring up to them, racing the pickup drivers. And far out on the high plains, the bicyclist explorer pedaling parallel to the immaculately ballasted main-line railroad track hears the soft beat of immense power coming up behind and sees the UPS train pass by, its twenty truck trailers atop ten flat cars pulled by two locomotives headed cityward at ninety miles an hour. The explorer pulls over, watches the caboose-less train rocket toward the horizon, and muses about a government that abandoned mail trains while a package-express company believes in the cold steel rail as the superhighway of the future. How did the people lose so much?

Somehow the explorer senses that the Postal Service has pulled back, somehow shrunk within itself, withdrawn its old offer of universal if unequal service. No longer does a Postal Service vehicle drive onto new privately owned ways, at least not to make regular, ordinary, first-class-stamp deliveries. Every new subdivision or office park now has a stainless steel cube of lockboxes where its driveway meets the public road. Once each day a letter carrier pulls up, opens the boxes, and deposits the mail, then pulls back onto the public pavement. Certainly the Postal Service brings Express Mail to the door, and the private companies deliver too. But the bicyclist understands the stainless steel lockboxes as the new termini of the public realm, and knows the new unwillingness of the Postal Service to venture far onto private ground, for venturing far from the public way costs money.

Instead of becoming more urban, more willing to open picket-fence gates and climb front stoops, the Postal Service grows daily more and more rural in its outlook, preferring that its carriers not only drive vehicles but stay in their vehicles. Once in a while the explorer stopped to identify wildflowers gracing a drainage ditch hears the faint sound of a car horn echoing across farm fields and guesses that some RFD carrier is delivering an Express Mail envelope to some farmyard and summoning someone, anyone, to walk out to the vehicle. The horn-blowing speeds the mail now just as it speeds the deliveries of the UPS driver, but the explorer wonders at the stainless steel lockboxes that are somehow as much a boundary as the decrepit wire fences along ancient railroad rights-of-way. If the mail carrier will not enter, or cannot enter, at least not ordinarily enter, who else may pass, who else can pass?

Four

Strips

WHAT HAPPENS WHEN ROADS WITHER? When grass grows not among the railroad ties but in the streets?

The explorer soon knows what the harried motorist misses until the motorist blows a tire or bends a rim in a pothole. Roads everywhere in the country crumble now, and the edges of pavement grow more ragged by the year. Even urban streets reveal a sort of fraying where pavement meets curbstone, where the subtle subsidence of storm-drain and manhole covers makes craters, where the long, thin, branching cracks that run parallel to the roadway and bunch together near the center line of pavement turn into crevices. Forced to the edge of pavement by automobiles and trucks, the explorer sees the margin of pavement in ways motorists never do. The explorer notes the storm drains choked with leaves and dirt, the pavement buckled by frost and snowplows, the myriad hot-top patches applied after slapdash water- and gas-main repair, the so-called cold-patch asphalt scaling from potholes scabbed over on winter days. And in the late spring, the explorer descries the seeds sprouting in the soil between pavement and curbstone, or the grass thrusting up through cracks inches away from thrumming automobile tires. Across much of rural, even small-town and suburban America, the explorer sees the slow drift of pine needles, crumbled leaves, and vine tendrils moving from shoulders long unmowed onto and across the asphalt. In city and country, the explorer knows the roadway ecosystem and knows that nature slowly retakes the road as it retook the railroad station platform decades ago.

Always highways create an artificial ecosystem of living things, one that in time overwhelms fragile blacktop. Pavement drains rainwater into storm drains sometimes, but usually onto shoulders, and the rainwater creates ecosystems dependent on it. Across semiarid regions, especially the High Plains, the explorer moves on the edge of the black, paralleling a two-foot-wide band of dark green, often rather lush vegetation. But six feet from the edge of asphalt, the deep green fades into paleness, then brown, for the scant rainfall collected along the edge of the pavement seeps only a few feet into the ordinary dry-soil ecosystem. In humid places, plentiful rainfall not only washes frequently over always-lush shoulders but fills and refills the ditches that line so many secondary and tertiary roads. In the ditches grow wetland plants alien to the upland a few feet away, and in the stagnant or slightly flowing water live the reptiles and amphibians long accustomed to the motor vehicles roaring past, just inches away, but not always careful to avoid being hit. Along ditch-lined roads, especially in spring, explorers walk as body counters, marveling at the carcasses of snakes and toads and salamanders.

Often the plants bordering the asphalt are exotic, strangers from other places down the road, sometimes from far away. Farm trucks roaring to market spill sorghum seed, and the sorghum sprouts along suburban roads; lawn-service trucks carrying away bamboo or other invasive plants like the imported five-foot-tall grass *Fragmenties* lose a bit of cargo from beneath flapping canvas, and here and there the foreign plants take route a few feet from the pavement, often quickly edging out indigenous species.

Occasionally highway departments mow the shoulder or berm, but as capital-improvement and maintenance budgets shrank after the 1960s, the mowing machines came less and less frequently, shrubs replaced grasses, and roots probed beneath pavement, then rose to buckle it. The explorer notices the withdrawal of shoulder maintenance because the explorer cannot ignore how quickly the roadside ecosystem invades the road, especially when maintenance and traffic both decrease, and how permanently the roadside ecosystem establishes itself. And the explorer knows that the roadside ecosystem of plants and animals prospers as another ecosystem withers.

HIGHWAYS AND WELL-TRAVELED roads produce an economic ecosystem, too, and always have. Bicyclists in the most rural regions of the original thirteen colonies still pedal past the once-lonely inns where travelers rested while coachmen changed horses; walkers in urban areas stride past hotels that replaced the hotels that replaced the hotels in which coach travelers delighted. Old inns remind the explorer that horses tired as well and sometimes needed replacement far from cities and villages and county seats. Most lonely inns became less lonely gasoline stations in the first years of the twentieth century, if their owners did not convert them to general stores or houses in the long decades when railroad travel emptied almost every long-distance road in the nation.

Explorers sometimes realize, after walking uphill for miles and beginning to think about a snack or lunch, that innkeepers often located inns where teamsters stopped to rest tired horses. Inns, rural general stores, old wood-frame gasoline stations still stand in places useful to tired walkers and tired horses. Explorers thinking about muscles today begin to discover ways muscle power shaped landscape in centuries past.

Consider the pail bail, nowadays called the handle of the bucket. Carry the pail and the bail arcs above the rim. Set down the pail and the bail falls sideways along the rim. Either way, the bail remains the same length. Such is the lesson of nineteenth-century farmers explaining road routing to impatient children sitting beside them in wagons creeping around a hill or mountain. Upright or flat along the rim, the bail remains the same length. But far better to let the horse follow a flat, curving route than one of the same length over a steep hill. Why tire the horse?

So the exploring walker or bicyclist understands the relationship of hills and muscles, and knows that even now businesses cluster at the base or top of hills, rarely midway along the grades. Where horses rested the explorer often rests, and sometimes finds a gasoline station or store occupying the site of some eighteenth- or nineteenth-century hostelry. But more likely the back-road explorer finds only a grown-over cellar hole or a massive elm shading lesser trees. Business moved to other places once Ford put the nation into flivvers.

By 1920, businessmen knew that travelers moved so frequently by automobile that only the most prosperous of downtowns would survive. Motorists wanted to park, to drive quickly between home and town, farm and village, city to city, to not get lost or mired in mud. As early as 1900, the first motorists learned to use League of American Wheelmen bicycling maps to plan their motorized routes, and learned to visit the country inns and taverns at which tens of thousands of bicyclists refreshed themselves in the stunningly popular first fifteen years of the bicycle fad, when the LAW became a major political action group agitating solely for road improvement. Year by year, local and state governments improved road signs, road-surface conditions, and bridges, then funded innovations like numbered routes and traffic signals adapted from railroads. As roads improved and cars became more reliable, motorists drove more and more miles with less and less deliberation, and merchants grasped what gasoline station owners knew. A roadside location with off-road parking meant greater and greater business.

The explorer on a bike sees the palimpsest of economic development simply because he or she moves from era to era effortlessly, sometimes cruising alongside the cars parallel parked in front of nineteenth-century storefronts, sometimes warily skirting cars angle parked in turn-of-the-century small-town main streets, then pedaling into more modern places. Just at the edge of most small towns, clinging still to the fringes of suburban train station-focused villages, stretching outward from great cities stand the highway-focused business districts built between 1920 and 1950 when the roads they still front were the main roads to everywhere. The explorer knows the commercial ecosystem of those decades by the way its buildings snuggle against the road, sometimes because owners built far too close to the road to begin with, but usually because highway departments subsequently widened roads as traffic thickened and trucks grew wider.

On old highways, gas stations and restaurants and furniture stores now sit so close to pavement that they remind the bicyclist that once traffic moved about twenty-five miles an hour, that motorists spotting a gasoline logo or ice cream stand had plenty of time to slow down and pull in, turning sharply into the shallow parking lots. Often the explorer sees the telltales of the era, the gasoline station with pumps set only ten feet in from the pavement, protected by no curbstone, and set only ten feet out from the station building itself, or the fast-food building shaped like a bottle or ice cream cone or coffeepot equally close to the road, often with a parking lot forcing customers to back perilously close to traffic when leaving.

ON SUCH ROADS the explorer probes casually and easily, for most motor vehicle traffic usually moves elsewhere, on wider roads a mile or so away, the roads lined with post–World War II shopping plazas, not malls. Plazas march along the wider roads usually numbered as state highways or business state highways, and plazas scream the importance of the 1960s car-driving woman shopper. Each plaza is anchored by a large store, often still a supermarket, its parking lot bordered on two other sides by lines of smaller stores selling everything from liquor to greeting cards to dry cleaning to sheets and pillowcases, its tenants advertised on a single overloaded sign planted at the edge of the road. The arrangement speaks of the spread of wide-open-space, West Coast–style retailing across the nation in the 1950s and 1960s.

Still busy, now often widened into five lanes, the plaza-lined highway, the commercial strip that in time inspired the creators of Las Vegas to build miles of casinos, owns a different time from old downtown shopping districts. It sleeps late on all but Saturday morning, awakening about ten and becoming busy only around noon, when lunch-hour-freed shoppers drive madly along it doing short-time errands, and nowadays buying lunch at any one of scores of specialized fast-foot outlets. Early afternoon brings out the retired couples and the stay-at-home mothers, and late afternoon attracts the high school kids not only working after school but shopping and hanging out and cruising around, enjoying the real world after indoor lessons. And evening brings the mad rush of home-bound shoppers doing more errands and, lately, buying meals ordered from car telephones, and the hesitant arrival of tourists and travelers struggling to find low-cost motels and lower-cost meals. As the remains of urban downtown retail districts lock up for the night, the commercial strip lights up, its millions of lights advertising that maternity shops and video stores and pizza parlors and fabric shops stay open until half past nine or later.

Despite their frenzy, commercial strips lose vitality now, something the walker or bicyclist discovers while exploring the back parking lots linked to each other in ways few motorists but all police officers know. Behind the glitter lurks the same deterioration so pronounced along the older retail ribbons, the deterioration resulting from the spawning of great regional malls in the late 1970s and early 1980s, and now from the coming of "category-buster" megastores demanding mall-size parking lots dedicated to their customers alone. Bicycle-riding explorers notice because they must. Every so often they need a new tube or tire or chain, and they know where they must pedal to find a bicycle shop.

Low-profit-margin businesses like bicycle shops cannot afford shopping mall locations and often can scarcely afford the rents in shopping plazas either. Moreover, bicycle shops need lots of floor space to display bicycles, just as furniture stores and mattress stores need lots of floor space too. So the bicycle-riding explorer needing a spare tube or updated component rides off away from the malls and the upscale plazas to the older strips where the muffler shops and radiator-repair businesses nestle against paint outlets and used sporting equipment emporiums. The bicyclist-explorer finds not only businesses slowly dying but businesses starting up, and sees the oddness of businesses strung out along highways but no longer dependent on business from motorists passing by. Instead the older commercial strips serve mostly customers making a special visit, and gradually signage becomes less and less important, less well designed, less well maintained, sometimes rusted and vine covered and topsy-turvy. No wonder the tourist or the motorist taking a different route cannot readily interpret the jam of signs and so often turns away from the older highways. Secondary shopping strips belong to those familiar with them, and business owners along them know that tourists stay on the interstate and rarely stray far from exit ramps when seeking motels or restaurants.

BEHIND ALMOST ALL commercial strips the explorer moves along the secret rights-of-way that few motorists find, that cheat all motorists, even the motorized police officer smelling trouble. A narrow ribbon snakes from one parking lot to another, through the trees on undeveloped sites, across the junk heaped up from aborted construction and demolition projects, always connecting one loading-dock area to another. Pedestrians use the ribbon. Sometimes homeless people scavenge in Dumpsters behind fast-food stores and sleep in warm cartons behind the appliance outlet and beg two-day-old bread from the back doorways of bakeries. Far more often teenagers use the corridor, hurrying back and forth between part-time jobs. They like to ride their mountain bikes along the corridor to avoid the crush of motor vehicle traffic on the highway a few hundred yards parallel, especially the danger and nuisance of cars forever turning from highway into parking lot and vice versa. Motorists no more notice the absence of pedestrians and bicyclists on commercial-strip highways than shopping mall customers are aware of the sorts of stores rarely found in malls. But the explorer glimpsing a half-dozen young riders vanishing behind a supermarket, then emerging from a parking lot barrier, walks or pedals away from the traffic jam toward the back of the strip, past the trailer truck waiting to unload, past the Dumpsters, onto the cognoscenti ribbon that twists and turns, sometimes becoming a two-rut cart path, now and then merging into a long-abandoned railroad right-of-way, then racing along a power-line right-of-way, then dropping into a litter-strewn, half-flooded parking lot studded with burned-out cars.

Everywhere the secret corridor intersects lesser routes at right angles, paths that vanish into scrub trees, paths that penetrate chain-link fences cut asunder ages ago. The narrow paths link residential neighborhoods with the secret corridor that snakes behind the backs of the commercial buildings, and frequently provide young children with shortcuts between grade schools and ball fields. Often the paths run at right angles through the wooded buffer strips some planning agencies mandate as screens between residential and commercial zones, giving any explorer a sense of moving through a narrow ribbon of wilderness. Sometimes the right-angle paths cross the oddest bodies of water imaginable—miles-long sloughs produced to drain the acres of parking lots abutting the highway, or to drain the highway storm drains themselves—or other bodies that to the explorer probing with an old stick seem to be deep-water remnants of nineteenth-century canals abandoned since the railroad victory of the 1870s. Bridges here and there dignify the right-angle paths, often bridges made of planks piled one atop another by several generations of children wanting to pass dry shod toward candy or baseball cards or CDs. And often No Trespassing signs and sometimes crude fences mark the far termini of the paths, the muddy or dusty places where paths fray into juniper hedges, board fences, swimming-pool enclosures, garages, vegetable gardens, all the constituent elements of a residential neighborhood.

The secret corridor proves an amazingly fast shortcut to any explorer determined to brush aside low-hanging branches and to risk broken glass and rusted wire. And it offers the probing and poking explorer another view of the chrome-and-glitter commercial strip, even of the regional mall, for it makes clear the stealth with which change comes. Build a new highway and the old strip withers, its buildings no longer leased to prime tenants, its landlords unable to resurface parking lots, spruce up facades. Build no new highways and the old strip withers too, as would-be shoppers drive elsewhere to avoid the traffic jams. Do nothing to accommodate larger trailer trucks making deliveries, and the truckers will pull over onto the unpaved ground, disturb then kill the plants, then set in motion erosion after every thunderstorm. Let the snowplow operators ram snow farther and farther beyond the pavement, and every spring reveals a plant-free gap on which teenagers can race ATVs and ancient motorcycles. Leave the graffiti on the back of the carpet store more than a day or two, and more graffiti appears, then more, until repainting the back of the store seems the only sensible thing to do until the landlord realizes that almost no one sees the mess, only the occasional employee stealing a cigarette by the back door, and the kids biking past, and the rare adult pedestrian pondering the wholesale abandonment of backdoor retail space.

Front-door retail space stands abandoned, too, sometimes merely month-to-month as For Rent signs fade into pallor, sometimes boarded up against vandals and arsonists, sometimes well insured and baiting vandals and arsonists. A building or two left derelict might be a mere eyesore, but the explorer realizes it stands as the first pronounced warning that economic trouble stalks the road, that the road has already failed a business or a handful of businesses, that more stand endangered.

The explorer who breaches the concrete barriers defending the abandoned parking lot often finds the clues explaining bankruptcy. Behind the building poke up the pipes of pollution-finding companies, and here and there rises the soil turned over by space-suited technicians pondering PCBs dumped long ago. In most states, commercial lenders demand site inspections before loaning money to would-be buyers, and explorers see the fruits of environmental sensitivity. Ecological responsibility sprouts up in test pipes and disturbed soil, but financial nightmare for property owners shows up best in pipes overgrown with wild morning-glory vines and test pits smothered in ragweed.

Once found, hazardous waste often requires wealth beyond imagination to clean up, and hazardous waste lies everywhere along the commercial strips, especially along the strips dating to the 1920s, when gas station mechanics poured oil into the ground and siding contractors dumped the asbestos shingles they could not burn. Exploring bicyclists riding the secret network behind commercial strips sometimes see the telltale signs, the drainage ditch floating in oil after a rain, the plants tinged bright yellow after droughts, the trees dead and dying after septic-tank work, the proliferation of *Fragmenties*, the alien import that flourishes in ground polluted with cadmium, lead, and other toxic metals.

So rapidly did heavy industry fail in the late 1960s and early 1970s that many contemporary shoppers forget the plating factory or small chemical works or dye plant that once stood where the shopping plazas pulse, or the junkyard on which developers built a regional mall. But the bicyclist wheeling along behind the plazas or the walker probing the sandy hillside beyond the mall parking lot glimpses the old Reo oil truck half buried in the eroded hillside and wonders what used to pay property taxes on the site. Oil and gasoline? Paints and solvents? Bleaching and tanning chemicals? Why a half mile beyond the mall does the old truck-repair dealership stand vacant year after year, or enormous trees with yellow-tinted leaves grow up in the abandoned fertilizer warehouse? Why does the dog loping along the path toward home shy away from the water seeping from the gravel bank behind the bank? Or as the explorer asks, sniffing the air suddenly, What is that sickly sweet smell? Most pedestrians or bicyclists exploring ordinary metropolitan landscape acquire fragmentary answers, learn a little bit of botany even if they never know the history or name of newly arrived plants that thrive in poison.

So Sunday morning finds the explorer sipping the last of the doughnut-shop coffee, wiping the honey-glazed doughnut stickiness on the grass, thinking at length about how much anyone can learn about American land development by meandering along and through a commercial strip. Investment money flows along the strips sometimes as obvious as a running brook, sometimes as concealed as complicated storm drains. And the explorer walking and looking and thinking realizes that the commercial strip is a sort of business ecosystem with its own dinosaurs, its own predators, its own survivors.

It is a remarkably accessible ecosystem, that much the explorer knows for certain. The customer is always welcome, always embraced by signs and parking lots and automatic doors. When the explorer stops for a minute or so to watch the commercial ecosystem, the explorer notices that the commercial strip is the portal through which toddlers and slightly older children enter the public realm. Long before a child learns about a schoolroom, the child learns how to behave in a fast-food restaurant and how to walk through a store, staying close to his or her own adults and not touching the merchandise. Accompanied by an adult with money to spend, every child is welcome in the ribbon of gleaming stores. The commercial strip and the shopping mall sweep a child into the world of the shopper, the easily accessible high road to acquisition, the road of private enterprise. So overwhelming is the welcome that highways without abutting retail businesses strike many children and many adults as dull.

Five

Interstate

Now and then the explorer finds the ramps leading to the interstate highway and realizes that contemporary people see the handiwork of the federal government most frequently now in the great highways that lace the country. To the explorer stopped atop a bridge arching over the twin ribbons of asphalt or concrete, the interstate highway becomes many things, an engineering marvel, almost an art form disappearing into the distance, perhaps a corridor of the imagination, always an expression of the power of the national government. But then the explorer looks a bit closer and begins to wonder, for the interstate highway rewards a bit of exploration.

No bicyclist rides the interstate highway, and few motorists zooming up entrance ramps think long about the political message implicit in the No Bicycles signs. The interstate highway system is by law and use a limited-access system, but *limited access* denotes two wholly separate issues. On the one hand, the term makes clear that abutters have no right to join the highway with their own land, no right to build gas stations or restaurants along the grassy margin and expect traffic to swerve onto new-paved parking lots. On the other, it emphasizes that the highway exists not for all citizens but only for those in vehicles suited to it, vehicles capable of the minimum speed of forty-five miles an hour. As the sign says, no bicyclists, no motor scooters, no self-propelled farm machinery, no horseback riders, no pedestrians, period. While all taxpayers contribute to its building and to its maintenance, although motorists pay even more through gasoline taxes, not all taxpayers are welcome on the special right-of-way.

In an era of civil rights, especially of individual rights guaranteed and reaffirmed by legislature and court, the ruthlessness with which government curtailed the freedom of travel of pedestrian, equestrian, and bicyclist demands at least fleeting attention. The explorer paused atop the overpass, looking down at the twin ribbons of pavement separated by median strip and abutted by mowed-grass shoulders and chain-link fences, feels no desire whatsoever to walk or bicycle among the speeding cars and trucks. But when the interstate highway bridge is the only bridge across a great river, the cross-country explorer grows as annoyed as when the foreign bicycle tourist, bicycle reassembled after some long flight into an American airport, discovers that only limited-access roads lead from airport to city, that the whole of the United States is therefore immediately inaccessible to any bicyclist leaving the airport baggage-concourse door. Explorers eventually discover that in many places, especially in cities, the interstate highway route is often the only route across a river, through industrial districts bordered by railroad yards, around airports.

Almost never do Americans realize the vagueness investing the very name of the limited-access highway system, let alone the origin of the system in Cold War murk. Legally the system is the Military and Interstate Highway System. It exists as a weapon, and like everything military, it exists for straightforward reasons, not pleasant ones perhaps, but straightforward nonetheless. Almost nothing of 1930s parkway design infuses the modern interstate highway. While a few states had experimented with limited-access roads designed to be free of trucks and to wind through scenic areas, by the late 1930s automobile manufacturers, the trucking and bus industries, and automobilists represented by auto clubs had banded together to advocate a new generation of highways like those the Germans had already developed for military reasons.

In the United States, perhaps the best prototype remains the Pennsylvania Turnpike, built on a never-completed main line railroad alignment—and once running through narrow tunnels built for trains—very late in the 1930s and carefully watched by military officers from the United States Army and from the German Wehrmacht. Already the Nazis understood the nation-binding, almost futuristic power of the limited-access autobahn, especially its cloverleaf interchanges and median-strip rest areas, and the German general staff knew clearly both the defensive and offensive capabilities of a limited-access, split-lane highway system designed for military vehicles. Built as cousins to each other, the Pennsylvania Turnpike and the autobahn attracted much military interest, for the highways seemed not only nearly bomb-proof but also perfectly useful as temporary runways for military planes. When the Pennsylvania Turnpike opened in 1940, then, it had military observers keen to witness its operation, and countless motorists anxious to drive along a road lacking a speed limit. By late 1941, when the phrase "going like sixty" described the half-in-, half-out-of-control feeling of driving a Ford sedan fast along a rural paved road, the *average* speed on the turnpike was ninety miles an hour, and while gasoline rationing meant a speed limitation during wartime, in the late 1940s the hundreds of thousands of GIs who had ridden tanks and trucks along the captured autobahnen knew the limited-access highway as the high-speed way of the future.

Nuclear-war technology and politics empowered Pentagon officers deeply respectful of the performance of German armored divisions along divided highways. A bigger armored vehicle might carry a nuclear-tipped guided missile, and if the massive vehicle roamed at will continuously over a special highway system, no Soviet missiles might target it. To be sure, the Pentagon put some missiles on trains, and 1950s railroad passengers sometimes noticed the military simulator car attached to the rear of passenger trains and joked that the Pentagon hid the whereabouts of the car by giving passenger-train timetables to Soviet spies, but always the general staff worried about the ease with which bombs sever tracks. So the Military and Interstate Highway System evolved first as a Third World War weapon, and for a solid legal reason too.

The Constitution forbids Congress from building roads because the framers of the Constitution understood road building as the first step toward creating a tyrannical, centralizing national government, and while the Supreme Court had years earlier decided that the right to *establish* roads stands implicit in the Constitution, no amount of loose interpretation could get past the explicit prohibition on building. Congress might declare a highway or rural cart path a post road, then, but it could not build a road unless the road served essentially as a weapon. So the Pentagon and civil engineers together designed the highway American motorists unthinkingly know, in all but congested urban areas a standard ribbon of well-divided multiple lanes bordered by grass and fences, in almost every case its grades and curvature as standardized as its overpass and underpass bridges.

As the military knew from repeated tries at destroying German and Japanese airfields, bombs that cratered paved surfaces left behind holes easily filled by bulldozers, so the new highway system would function well in conventional wars. Beyond that, studies of atom bomb damage in Japanese cities demonstrated that the new highway could withstand even nuclear hits, and that whatever damage might be done by A-bombs, even H-bombs, the Army Corps of Engineers could put right in a day or two, radiation excepted. Moreover, the five-mile-long straight stretches of highway across the High Plains made perfect secondary landing strips for B-52 bombers.

By the early 1950s, planners in the Strategic Air

Command knew that Soviet missiles would almost certainly destroy air force bomber bases, but that aircraft returning from first strikes might find safety, fuel, and more bombs cached alongside the Military and Interstate Highway System. So from the start, no power lines bordered the new highways, and except in a few places where federal authorities merged existing turnpikes into the new system, broad shoulders of mowed grass, not even ornamental plants, bordered the pavement.

Few motorists nowadays realize the relationship between aircraft design and highway design, but bicyclists exploring back roads know the rare thrill of seeing Wyoming highway troopers temporarily stopping highway traffic while an immense B-52 practices emergency landings a half mile away on the interstate. Only rarely do motorists ask why the military reserve units take over entire interstate highway rest stops or now and then pull over en masse in deep cuts or speed up when crossing bridges. Only a handful of rural families know that military interventions in Central America, the Persian Gulf, even Somalia often mandate the temporary closing of some stretch of isolated interstate highway abutting a major Marine Corps or other base. Almost never does the automobile-insulated public notice the massive military vehicle that at night moves along the Military and

Interstate Highway surrounded by state police cars, the vehicle still testing clearances and curves, the vehicle still swathed in Cold War despair and preparedness, the vehicle that sleeps in the daytime behind low-price motels when its operators cannot reach a military base, the parked and silent vehicle the bicyclist-explorer passes before lounging deputy sheriffs and coffee-sipping state troopers can turn and wave and shout.

Domestic politics shaped the Military and Interstate Highway System too, of course, but 1950s intent lies camouflaged by the word *interstate*. Big-city politicians knew that few rural taxpayers would subsidize an inter-city highway system, especially a system that limited rural access to widely spaced interchanges and cut swaths across thousands of miles of farmland. Calling the system *interstate* proved a touch of genius, however, for it made the system seem equally useful to all citizens, rural, suburban, and urban, and it finessed the constitutional issue: Congress built the system as a weapon, as a military highway, because it feared the enduring power of the constitutional prohibition against building ordinary roads.

But almost immediately, rural and small-town residents discovered that the new highway system linked city centers, and that entire regions of many states, especially lightly populated western states, got

nothing from the new system that ran straight between cities, sometimes between cities in adjacent
states. Indeed the new system sucked business away
from old state highways and country crossroads to the
rare interchanges at which long-distance motorists
stopped for gasoline, a quick meal, maybe a hotel
room. Once again, the federal government did to
rural America what it had done with the Post Office,
and even now the explorer sees here and there the
signs of deliberate civil disobedience, the tire-made
ruts of some driver who entered the interstate highway system by slamming his or her truck into four-
wheel-drive and roaring up the grassy shoulder.

Bicyclists can ride along but not on the interstate
highway, often discovering the frontage roads that
parallel the highways across hundreds of miles of
rural countryside and through miles of dense urban
fabric. Rural frontage roads are often dirt, or dirt
lightly oiled or tarred against dust, and they rise and
dip and curve far more actively than the sedate highway beyond the fence and mowed-grass berm. Often
connecting one county highway crossing over or
under the interstate with another five or ten miles
away, the rural frontage road sometimes sweeps
down close enough to the highway that the explorer
can see the oddities invisible at sixty-five miles an
hour.

For example, the backs of many great interstate highway green signs loom scarred with graffiti scrawled or carved by hitchhikers shaded from summer sun or by hunters trespassing along the drainage ditches dividing mowed grass from the scrub that grows along the fences, by the rural homeless who often camp a few hundred yards away, beyond the hole cut in the chain-link fence. Unless they break down near one of the green signs, interstate motorists never see the backs of the signs, or glimpse the tiny metal markers erected to delimit paving and repaving zones, to bound different plantings of grasses and wildflowers, to announce to highway workers that here begins an air force emergency landing strip.

In cities, few motorists ride frontage roads for long, knowing them to link interchanges and serve mostly the truckers making deliveries in industrial zones. Now and then, usually in traffic jams caused by collisions, stopped motorists realize that local fire and police departments use the frontage roads as alternative parallel routes, but only the explorer can know the shadows beneath all elevated urban highways, especially beneath the federal highways that plowed through cities in the 1960s serving as camouflaged urban renewal, what 1960s grass-roots political activists began calling "black removal" or "poor removal."

Weaving in and out of traffic, mindful of broken glass and the nails that litter the edges of frontage roads rarely traveled by citizens focused on urban aesthetics, noting the homeless roosting high up on the bridge abutments, the bicyclist-explorer discovers the dark view from the urban frontage road. Beneath the elevated interstate highway lie the lots to which dented tow trucks tow illegally parked cars, lots filled with piles of sand, great stacks of concrete lane barriers, heaps upon heaps of shattered asphalt and concrete and rusted reinforcing rod surrounded by derelict construction machines. Beneath the elevated highway stand disused construction-site trailers, long-parked trailer-truck trailers, dozens of buses with every window long smashed. Beneath the elevated highway march the four-foot-high piles of dirt and litter emptied in perfect rows from three-wheel street-sweeping machines, piles awaiting pickup by loaders and dump trucks that seem never to arrive. Everywhere beneath elevated interstate highways blossom makeshift dumps, great clutches of abandoned cars and burned-out cars, the former often occupied as homes by the homeless, the latter serving as unofficial Dumpsters and toilets. Beneath the elevated highway the exploring bicyclist finds the homes never visited by the United States Census, the clusters of cardboard cartons, sheet-metal boxes, construction-timber lean-tos, and automobile hoods that comprise the turn-of-the-millennium American jungle.

In the Great Depression railroad passengers knew about jungles. Tramps and whole families displaced by economic calamity "jungled up" just outside city limits, often in the dense growth of sumac or spruce that shaded the sun and broke the winter gales, usually near a river or creek useful as a sewer, if not for drinking water. Romanticized and criticized, flavored by mulligan stew and scented by creosoted wood alight in a rusted-out oil drum, home to the poor, the ex-convicts, the would-be train wreckers and mail-car robbers, the hobo jungle lingers in the memory of any explorer trudging along the weed-grown urban rails, wheeling carefully along the footpath linking active tracks with warehouses. But the new jungles flourish in shadows, away from trees, under cover of the federal interstate highway system.

Forbidden to trespass on the interstate highway, the exploring bicyclist approaches every city along frontage roads and decayed secondary highways crossing regions long since sliced by interstate highway politics and now almost pickled. While the old, sidewalk-bordered highways meandered through urban industrial and residential neighborhoods, the elevated interstate highway divided neighborhoods, making cross streets into long, dark, echoing tunnels, demolishing great swaths of structure, but above all, dead-ending a great many city streets.

Sometimes the explorer walking in the maze made by converging interstate highways smiles at the stream of traffic stopped far above and knows the privilege of walking into almost secret enclaves. The explorer sees redbrick factories cut off at frontage roads like slabs of cheese or notices entire factory complexes split in half by the elevated highway, and finds the diners that serve the factory workers at lunchtime. The explorer emerges from cavernous tunnels beneath the interstate highway into the sunlight of genuine surprise, finding anything from vibrant immigrant neighborhoods filled with outdoor restaurants proffering amazing arrays of food to warehouse districts offering wholesale prices on anything from garden equipment to magazines to repossessed automobiles to water-damaged artist supplies. High above the explorer, stopped in traffic, fume hundreds, sometimes thousands of people anxious to arrive at interesting places, and unable to see over the guardrails into the myriad of intriguing places the explorer discovers with amazement. The great interstate highway acts as a sort of fence, and only the explorer learns the many gateways through it.

Six

Enclosures

EVERYWHERE THE EXPLORER MOVES, he or she discovers fences and slowly realizes that fences are the unmentioned high-tech device of the last years of the twentieth century. Fences fence out, and fences contain, but only the explorer paralleling them and occasionally pausing to scrutinize them sees the ruthlessly efficient divvying up of the country.

From the very first settlement, colonists struggled to keep cattle, hogs, and other livestock either secured inside pastures and paddocks or else securely outside cornfields, gardens, and other planted ground. From Pennsylvania northward, colonists fenced *in* livestock and elected hog reeves—a reeve is a gatherer—to capture wandering animals and intern them in outdoor pounds until owners paid fines.

(While the ancient *shire reeve* is now contracted to *sheriff*, rural New Englanders still elect livestock reeves.) South of Pennsylvania, colonists enclosed crops *against* livestock permitted to wander anywhere else, to graze along roadsides, to roam deep into forest until rounded up by the slaves—literally the cowboys—and branded at central sites like the Cowpens, which gave its name to a Revolutionary War battlefield. Westward expansion moved the two attitudes into the Mississippi Basin and beyond, and brought newcomer neighbors into bitter disputes. Fencing acrimony helped start the Civil War, and in later decades in the Far West it divided northern-attitude farmers from southern-attitude ranchers, and now pits ranchers against retirees, ski-resort owners, even yuppies gentrifying mining towns.

Once railroad companies learned that full-grown bulls sometimes derailed trains, steel-and-wood locomotive cowcatchers notwithstanding, fences soon bordered every railroad corridor in the North and South. However, rural dirt roads away from New England, New York, and Ohio often lacked fences into the 1920s, forcing motorists into terrifying collisions with grazing horses and steers. Travelers on horseback and in wagons expected confrontations with wandering horses and pigs, but not until automobilists began colliding with valuable farm animals did state legislatures enact "herd laws," mandating that farmers fence in all their livestock. Decades later, at the start of the interstate highway era, the federal government mandated that the high-speed roads be fenced at public expense, especially where great herds of beef cattle might stray onto the roadway. Only in the 1960s, as the interstate highway reached across the plains, did New Mexico end its long-standing "free-range" tradition and accept the fences that bordered its new interstate highways, but even now motorists in Maine discover the horror of hitting moose and long-distance truckers in Idaho wreck their vehicles after striking bears. Most roads stand unfenced against intruders, animals or otherwise, but most motorists still presume farmers contain their livestock.

EXPLORERS IMMEDIATELY LEARN something about the astounding regionalism of traditional rural fences by walking or riding through countryside settled generations ago by pioneers from different eastern regions, pioneers whose descendants still maintain or at least tolerate fencing types dating to colonial experiments. New England stone walls evolved first as linear rock piles, the aftermath of clearing land of tree stumps and stones, and until the 1850s worked as fences only when topped with rails split from logs. Southern fences were rarely made of stone but usually consisted of split rails interlaced horizontally, and snaked across the ground without benefit of upright posts. New England walls and southern snake fences moved westward, separated by the post-and-rail fences devised by New York, New Jersey, and Pennsylvania colonists, and mingling in the eastern Mississippi Valley as sectionalism flared into civil war.

Pioneering in the rock-free, nearly treeless High Plains demanded new fencing types, and the invention of barbed wire mounted on metal stakes changed cattle ranching from a Wild West free-for-all into a prosaic, efficient operation based on water holes and corrals. Barbed-wire fencing spread eastward, too, supplanting wood rails in all but the poorest and richest regions, and stimulating the development of woven-wire fencing in different meshes from the chicken-wire type favored by poultry farmers to the tough large-square-grid type used by hog farmers. The voracious demand for metal fencing by railroad companies and subsequent overproduction drove down the price, and farmers quickly abandoned traditional wood types. As farming decayed in poor-soil regions or regions undergoing suburbanization, farmers merely nailed wire fence along decaying wood fences or else stapled the wire directly to trees.

The fences that seduce the explorer into stopping and pondering today fence few livestock in or out and protect little in the way of crops. Instead the fences that demand attention are those that mark property boundaries and deter people, fences that smack of the heritage of railroad fences.

From the 1890s onward, careful suburban home-owners fenced their property with metal fences, sometimes woven-wire, more often chain-link attached to metal poles, all galvanized against rust. The Panic of 1893 that set so many out-of-work men roaming across the country and riding freight trains sparked the fencing in of suburban backyards, especially those that abutted railroad tracks tramped by tramps. In the 1920s, the easygoing security following the purchase of large house lots caused many home-owners to forgo fencing, but the depression, and especially the Lindbergh baby kidnapping, set off a second orgy of residential fence building, this time with fences having almost no agricultural anteced-ents. Chain-link ruled back- and side yards, and often ran along front-lawn edges; frequently the chain-link fencing towered six or eight feet tall if backyards abutted any unofficial long-distance route like rail-road tracks, rivers, or power-line rights-of-way.

Planted with lilacs, or in backyards serving as trellises for climbing peas and beans, the metal fences not only defended against the homeless, the beggar, and the criminal but kept others from trespassing visually. In depression parlance, *lookers* or *peepers* designated anyone, even otherwise respectable families, out for a walk or a drive in neighborhoods far more wealthy than their own. Homeowners argued that such people must be kept at a distance lest they pick flowers or picnic on private greensward; in reality they irritated the well-to-do, who were concerned that by watching they might in time succumb to socialist ideas about the inequities of wealth.

By the late 1930s, the relaxation of backyard social mores—or deviancy, in the eyes of many conservative Americans—prompted at least the planting of lilacs along the metal fences, if not the erecting of solid wood fences inside the metal ones. As more and more health-conscious Americans sunbathed in little or nothing behind their houses, as more and more women decided to drink a glass of beer outdoors, families began building fences that stopped more than trespassing. The tall brick walls, sometimes topped with shards of glass set into concrete, the thick osage-orange hedges laced with chain-link fencing, even the eight-foot-tall board fences painted white or dark gray served to block views. Once fenced in, housewives knew a relaxing freedom that seems almost quaint today. No longer did they worry that neighbors might find them reading movie magazines instead of hanging out laundry, or concern themselves about male motorists seeing them in prototypical bikinis. Trees, shrubs, and above all fences screened out probing eyes, especially the probing eyes of male transients, of male *strangers*.

Despite the social uniformity so many 1950s urban observers found in new-made suburbs of ranch-style houses, homeowners quickly erected fences as effective in stopping the eye as the tall walls so many built in the 1930s. By the early 1960s, suburban America sprouted cedar-screen fencing everywhere, the at-least-eye-level fences intended to stop Peeping Toms from peeping. Cedar-screen fences are essentially walls of six-foot-high cedar pickets nailed side by side so closely that the pickets block vision. While the cedar-screen fences stand at one end of the residential fencing tradition that extends backward into the early 1890s, they differ in one intriguing way. Unlike the steel fencing and brick walls of earlier residential privacy thinking, the cedar-screen fences rot.

Despite creosote, green-tinted preservative, and liberal applications of crankcase oil, the cedar posts supporting the six-by-six or six-by-eight panels of half-round cedar pickets simply decay. And the great panels that act like sails catching the wind slowly begin working the weakening posts back and forth. The explorer walking or pedaling alongside cedar-screen fencing sees the pipes, lengths of angle iron, and even broomsticks homeowners pound alongside rotten cedar posts, sees the rope and wire cable stretched from one secure post to another, sees the coat-hanger-wire supports linking posts and solid shrubbery. An extraordinary number of Americans want fences that screen out the public eye, but apparently can no longer afford—or will no longer afford—to properly repair the fences or replace them when they deteriorate. The explorer knows what any trespassing-bent child knows: The rickety fences are easily penetrated, simply by pulling off a handful of pickets. But the explorer knows a secret too, a secret pedestrians and motorists never imagine.

Depending on the spacing of the pickets that seem at first glance to make a solid wall, the bicyclist-explorer can pedal at some magic speed that makes the fence transparent. Usually about eleven miles an hour does the trick. At that speed the explorer can see through the fence almost as though the fence had disappeared. At a speed that runners and pedestrians rarely reach for long and so slow that few motorists ever attempt it, the explorer rides effortlessly, and secretly, screened from observation by the fences intended to block views, spying on what the fences surround.

But why build screen fences? What secrets hide behind the rickety fences? Thong bikinis? An unregistered automobile dripping oil? Enough dogs for a kennel permit? A quiet manufacturing business forbidden by zoning regulations? A marijuana patch? The bicyclist-explorer rides and looks and learns that fences hide nothing extreme, nothing illegal, nothing particularly out of the ordinary.

The explorer afoot looks a bit more deliberately perhaps and sees nothing particularly out of the ordinary either. Seeing the nothing, seeing what is not in the landscape, empowers the explorer, because discerning what is not in the picture enables the explorer to make connections. The explorer who slows down or stops for a few moments to look around, to catalog what appears to be absent, becomes the connoisseur of noticing. Most people look around and see things. The explorer looks around and sees the patterns and revelations disclosed by things absent. When most people notice fences at all, they tend to think of them as blocking movement. The explorer discovers something different.

The explorer determines that the fences mark property boundaries, mark "turf," by defining the limits of public gaze. The front lawn is open to view, part of the scene, a contribution to the public landscape. But all other domestic outdoor property, at least away from farms, belongs in a private realm, a realm protected from casual public observation by fences that prove neither insurmountable nor opaque, but that seem so at first glance. The fences mark the last refuge of outdoor private identity, of individual and family identity, by insisting that backyard private life ought not be public spectacle, no matter how dull and insipid the spectacle might prove.

In neighborhoods where criminals take more than glances, or where property owners think they do, fences become secure against penetration. In such places only a handful of homeowners attempt to screen out prying eyes by lacing vinyl strips through the chain-link fencing. Instead most homeowners here seem to welcome views into backyards, if only to make would-be thieves aware that the backyards lack anything remotely worthy of theft, not even rusted gas grills. But since the backyards offer access to back doors and windows, the fences surrounding the backyards are solid indeed and often topped with the farmer's favorite fencing, barbed wire.

Yet the barbed wire used by cattle ranchers and dairy farmers is far less hurtful than that stretched atop metal fences around so many burglar-threatened backyards. Homeowners and storekeepers and factory superintendents favor what the trade calls "vicious" barbed wire, with barbs three times as long as those the rancher or farmer uses. Two, three, sometimes even four strands of barbed wire reach along the tops of chain-link fence and often amid and above the barbed-wire spiral coils of razor-edged concertina wire. Since the great urban riots of the mid-1960s, fencing and burglar-alarm installation have proven extraordinary growth industries, and sometimes the explorer discerns their eerie symbiosis. Here and there, even in serene suburban alleys, the explorer sees the theft-prevention wire stretched taut between the concertina coils and knows without reading the aluminum warning sign that to climb the fence means to set off noise.

Alarms make noise, and the probing explorer sees the noisemakers and other gadgets. Sometimes the horns and bells are deliberately obvious, fixed to building facades as visible indicators of the microcircuitry within. But often the alarm systems are less obtrusive. The explorer glimpses the silver metallic tape edging panes of window glass, the fine wire across the insides of door windows, the strobe lights mounted under eaves. And, of course, the signs. Everywhere away from public facades, homes and businesses blossom with signs, often tiny ones stuck to windows, sometimes large ones riveted to back doors or wired to backyard fences; the signs warn would-be intruders that indoors are devices that summon Authority. Other signs, often older and rusted, warn of dogs.

Fences keep watchdogs within, and out of trouble. The explorer quickly learns the meaning of the grassless, muddy track paralleling wire fences, and knows that the slightest noise, the merest cough or comment, brings a dog from somewhere to the border of private property. Rottweilers and Dobermans, German shepherds and enormous mongrels, once in a while a pair of giants guided by a diminutive but wildly yapping poodle—all pursue the explorer moving deeper and deeper into industrial park space, past the sprawling junkyard, the construction-equipment rental business, the used-car lot, the agricultural-machinery auction barns, down behind the welding shop, the auto-body shop, the foundry. Watchdogs burst from plastic doghouses, sheet-metal doghouses, even from one-piece styrene plastic doghouses emblazoned with aggressive names.

Motorists rarely see the dogs, for the fences extend from both rear corners of buildings nestled against parking lots and public ways, but the explorer moving along alleys or riding the crooked footpath along drainage canals hears the barking and howling lurch from lot to lot, skipping over lots defended by electronic alarms or dozing watchmen, reaching far off toward residential areas filled with fat, slothful dogs ready to bark a bit too. Wherever the fences change from wood to metal, wherever streetlights shift from white to orange, wherever alleys open on backs of buildings defended with bars and steel doors, the explorer is barked along by dogs lunging at chain-link fencing, at dogs who not only warn of intrusion but deal with intruders.

AT WHAT POINT does the explorer become someone else, perhaps the self-appointed inspector of safety and good order? How does the explorer differ from the would-be burglar casing the back of a factory, a warehouse? The explorer stops, sees the padlock hanging open since Friday afternoon, and wonders about pushing open the gate and walking into the factory yard, then walks on, knowing that trespass is wrong. Or the explorer sees the starlings nesting in the box marked "alarm" and guesses the box is a fake. How hard would it be to trespass, to burgle, to steal? How does one get to that strange building surrounded by metal fencing, if not by following the brook to the drainage ditch, then crawling along the ditch under the straddling fence? And suddenly the explorer realizes that he or she is indeed someone else, the rare person who knows that crime is not nearly as widespread as the television news asserts. The explorer who looks around at fences and gates understands that homes and businesses are often only perfunctorily protected, that the landscape demonstrates a stupendous faith in honesty.

The bicyclist-explorer who rides all day from rural

places through suburbs into urban residential areas and finally into the very heart of the urban industrial zone rides from metal fences that contain powerful animals to decorative wood or wire fences that gently mark boundaries and support climbing roses to wood-panel fences that screen out Peeping Toms to metal fences that defend against burglars to metal fences sunk in concrete that contain animals far more dangerous than the cows and horses the bicyclist passed at daybreak. And the bicyclist now and then sees disaster waiting to happen—the sagging fence at the end of the cow pasture, the eight-foot-tall cedar-screen fence blowing gently in the breeze, the snow-plow-damaged warehouse fence open almost enough to let the slavering Doberman through.

In the end, however, the explorer knows that the proliferation of fences has less to do with livestock containment or theft prevention than with the shrinking of American tolerance. Why shouldn't the public see into backyards if backyard behavior proves dull and commonplace? Why erect the expensive fences that rot? What has happened to the public realm, the public eye, the tolerant gaze?

Certainly the public trust endures. Away from cities march mailboxes alongside every public road, the mailboxes served six days a week by the 750,000 rural letter carriers employed by the United States Postal Service. And all, every last one, can be locked with a padlock, a padlock having keys held by carrier and homeowner. But how often does the explorer find a padlocked mailbox? Once in a thousand miles? Ever? Day after day, the carriers drive their routes, placing in lonely mailboxes the bills and letters and social security checks and automobile registration forms and income-tax refunds and love letters that everyone takes for granted. Who robs the unlocked box? Who opens it and riffles through the mail, then skulks off to spy elsewhere? In a land divided by fences that block the public gaze, what explains the rural and suburban trust in the unlocked RFD box mounted atop a maple or cedar post? Do Americans fence themselves to keep their images from being stolen? Do all the fences scream loudest about the gaze that steals? Or do they indicate something about trespasses not forgiven?

The bicyclist-explorer who rides from city to suburb to small town to rural county notices the shift in mail delivery and knows now that where the RFD carrier cannot travel, the public is no longer welcome. The RFD carrier and the bicyclist alike know the creeping extension of *limited access*, know the deeper meaning of *exclusive,* know the fast-growing proclivity of like-minded Americans to jungle up at the outermost edge of the outermost suburbs and throw around themselves intruder-proof fencing.

Past the stainless steel lockboxes that almost

warn away the federal government, around the lowered gates that keep out burglars, tourists, and bewildered motorists, the bicyclist-explorer trespasses innocently onto private roads designed to discipline unthinking guests driving in well-ordered private space. Sometimes a sign warns of speed bumps or—far more potent—speed dips, signaling the explorer that here rules an order unknown in the public realm. In fiefdoms labeled *adult community* or *private domain* or *private community,* the explorer finds the American equivalent of the Japanese *joka-machi,* the ancient town walled against warlords, marauders, and criminals too powerful for roaming samurai warriors. The explorer glimpses a whole built environment, a whole way of living imported not so much from Europe as from Asia. In the *joka-machi* residents are free, free even from visits by United States Postal Service letter carriers, but caged too. Perimeter fences bound the private communities, walling out undesirable would-be visitors and walling in everyone who belongs.

At the end of the century, some 130,000 such communities dot the Republic, home to nearly thirty million citizens physically closed off from wider environments, sometimes even from the explorer afoot or atop a bicycle. Ranging in size and type from a score of 1970s mobile homes circled wagon-train-like behind chain-link fence to several hundred spectacular houses or paired condos nestled in hilly forest and greensward a half mile from the nearest public way, the private communities share only fences as their common denominator.

Islands set within larger built environments, so frequent in parts of the South and the West that the bicyclist-explorer rides through entire archipelagos of them, the enclaves not only exclude the public but mandate behavior within. Residents of the gated, fenced, and patrolled communities behave according to rigidly enforced rules, repeated breaking of which leads to fines and other punishments, including banishment. At first, the explorer easily misses the sweeping majesty of rules, especially in the upscale enclaves impeccably maintained by professional gardeners, horticulturists, painters, and even interior designers. But the explorer walking or cycling past the guard post—often unmanned but definitely designed to be manned immediately if trouble threatens from beyond the fence—into pristinely designed space eventually realizes that the aesthetic harmony of the enclaves evolves not only from original design but from eternal control.

The private roads follow the natural contours of the land, but no cars park on the shoulders. The pleasing palette of exterior color is landscape-architect-chosen but endures because no homeowner can choose beyond its narrow range of colors. The natural planting blends with imported exotics across the whole site, and no homeowner can plant any shrub or tree beyond those listed on a master list and furnished from a single well-run nursery. No tree-of-heaven clumps interrupt the azaleas. No homeowner can place anything but an automobile in his or her driveway, and some enclaves forbid even half-afternoon driveway projects like painting a small boat or cleaning a newly bought antique table. Even on the land the homeowner personally owns, the half acre or so that surrounds each individual unit, the rules prohibit the erecting of hammocks or umbrellas or children's play equipment or bird feeders, or else mandate that the objects be selected from items chosen by architect and owners' association in concert. And given that most acreage belongs to the association, and that most of the acreage exists to be looked at mostly, perhaps jogged through, maybe played golf upon, the acreage blends seamlessly into a finely crafted environment.

Fenced enclaves stand always as immense cul-de-sacs. No trucks rumble through them and destroy the pavement. No automobile traffic shortcuts across them, bringing noise and danger to children riding tricycles. Never do utility companies load enclave poles with cables intended to serve communities far away, for the enclaves usually lack poles and always have dead-end service anyway. Never, ever do local and state highway authorities arrive to widen roads. Whatever the fenced communities fence out, they fence in stasis.

Inside the fence, in the immense cul-de-sac, change occurs only according to the program. New neighbors by definition accept the greater ideals and restrictions of the enclave, for they choose to live in the enclave. Storms now and then fell an aging tree, but no one paints a house bright purple or strands a half-wrecked pickup truck on cinder blocks. And supposedly, no resident arrives home to find that burglars have stolen family heritage or the laptop computer on which promotion depends.

On any day, the explorer can probe past the enclave gates without pause and without fear, because the gates exist to stop motorists. Only the rare enclave turns away pedestrians and cyclists. Enclave residents assume the explorer is harmless, out for cardiovascular exercise, out to lose weight, maybe just out. In the great enclaves spreading across the land, the explorer discovers something. Pedestrians and bicyclists are not perceived as threats.

Intrusion, incursion, invasion, all continuously imperil and preoccupy the enclave residents ostensibly secure inside their state-of-the-art perimeter. Many enclaves resemble garrisons designed by army officers. The richer the inhabitants, the more likely the enclave sits in undulating terrain camouflaged by woods, often by sapling woods planted to camouflage the narrow roadway intersecting with the public way. Sometimes a sign announces the name of the enclave but more often only a number sandblasted into a boulder. Almost always the narrow road takes a sharp turn a few hundred feet in from the intersection, making any prying, long-distance view impossible. Just around the turn, far enough into the deciduous woods to be more or less invisible even in winter, but often carefully screened with white pines, junipers, and other fast-growing conifers whose green works as well in winter as in summer, the explorer finds the perimeter fence.

Away from resort and urban areas, the residential enclave almost always tosses away some of its acreage as no-man's-land, dropping it into a limbo between public road and perimeter fence. The buffer or camouflage zone remains privately owned, to be sure, but no one uses it, at least no humans. Instead the zone becomes a sort of trace for wildlife deflected by the perimeter fence and perfectly comfortable walking or scurrying parallel to public roads. Free from harassment by motorists and pedestrians, and scarcely bothered by residents of the enclave inside the fence, the deer and raccoons and other animals discover that enclave building creates miles of well-forested roadside interrupted more or less regularly by narrow private roads. The motorist breezing along the well-wooded public ways, even the motorist commuting along them day after day, often misses the extensive residential development carefully camouflaged and almost serendipitously pleasing ecologists and conservationists and bird-watchers anxious to help indigenous wildlife threatened by technological society.

Roadkill intrigues the explorer. Motorists flick steering wheels to avoid running over the carcasses that litter roads abutted by camouflaged enclaves, but the explorer slows and sometimes stops, noticing not only the bodies on the asphalt but those resting in the sand and scrub of the shoulder. Early in the morning, sometimes even on weekday afternoons, the explorer moves so silently as to surprise at work the scavengers from the forest buffer. Lying on the pavement or lying where they crawled and died in the fitful cover of grass or the damp of the drainage ditch, the dead squirrels and chipmunks and turtles and snakes and possums and raccoons and cats and dogs and starlings and robins attract the scavengers who patrol the roadsides. Crows and ravens and even hawks and owls rip and tear the carcasses, but sometimes larger animals look up as the explorer approaches, then dart into cover. Feral cats, skunks, fishers, and coyotes work the wooded roads abutting the enclave perimeters, finding roadkill a regular supplement to ordinary diets. For all their detailing in immaculate lawns, swept-away leaves, and fertilized shrubbery, private residential enclaves somehow enhance wild animal habitats, or else their camouflage perimeters encourage existing wild animals to venture near public roads in a way that suburban front lawns do not. And since some enclaves forbid the keeping of cats and dogs for reasons of noise and mess and allergies, at least those enclaves free of subsidized predators become haphazard nature preserves, the home of the hawks the explorer sees circling above rush-hour highways, waiting for the morning roadkill.

Stopped for a moment, maybe a minute, maybe longer to sit and rest and think, the explorer hits upon an odd dichotomy in American culture. No one picks up roadkill, except to dispose of it, maybe in a shallow grave. The chipmunk or turtle lies dead, then flat, then flatter, dried against the asphalt. But at the beach, everyone picks up carcasses. Every parent urges every toddler to pick up shells; every adult picks up the lobster claw, the whole crab carapace tossing in the wavelets. What makes the dead turtle shell different from the quahog shell? How is the leather-like dead snake unlike the dead lobster? Does exo-skeleton alone make carnage special? What does it mean when a self-styled vegetarian admits to eating fish? The explorer who muses about roadkill confronts the vagueness with which contemporary people classify degrees of "aliveness," and the greater vagueness about what is really dead. Autumn leaves, no matter how brilliantly colored, fall to the ground dead, but the tree lives. The odd feather blowing in the wind is fine for toddlers to grasp, but no one considers plucking a dead bird and handing the feathers to a child. Fish, leaves, feathers, all cross the imagination of the explorer exploring.

Such is the meandering nature of ordinary exploration, ordinary poking and probing in ordinary space.

Riding from one enclave to another, zigzagging along the ill-paved secondary public road that links one portion of suburban sprawl to another, the bicyclist-explorer understands the *joka-machi* not only as cage but as vision, the experimental prototypical community not of tomorrow, not of racial or ethnic diversity, but of homogeneity of interest, income, and behavior. Aesthetics offer reasons why so many inhabitants of enclaves love them: The enclaves are, after all, holistically designed and maintained in gentle if often boring ways. Scale offers reasons why architects and landscape architects love them: A residential enclave, a *planned residential development*, means a fat design fee, a far, far fatter design fee than the sum total of hard-earned single-family design fees for the same number of residences in ordinary landscape. And the land left in camouflage and certainly not given over to lawns only introduces reasons why local planning boards and the Audubon Society so often favor the walled enclaves that trick motorists into thinking they still drive through second-growth forest wilderness and offer wildlife corridors, patches, and edges that encourage movement and population increase at the expense of roadkill. However, what really seems to drive the quickening rush to residential enclaves is nostalgia, and mixed-up nostalgia at that, one blended from eighteenth-century landscape images and early twentieth-century suburban aesthetics.

At the turn of the twenty-first century, people are nostalgic for greensward, for the open meadows of the half-imagined rural past, for the lawns of so many images ranging from mid-nineteenth-century Currier & Ives lithographs to the carpetlike lawns advertised by fertilizer companies. Today the typical suburban house-on-a-lot endures as a miniature farm, a sort of living mausoleum of 1840s-style farming. A fruit tree or two recalls the orchard. The patch of vegetable garden reminds everyone of great fields once planted to tomatoes, cabbage, peppers, potatoes. The backyard, usually more or less fenced, is vestigial pasture, roamed by the substitute livestock, a dog and a cat. And the front yard, the lawn so carefully fertilized and mowed but never otherwise used, recalls the meadow, the source of hay.

Lawns fascinate Americans because they recall the agrarian origins of the country, particularly the near self-sufficiency and tolerance prized by farm families before the Civil War and subsequent heavy industry swept away rural quiet and agricultural time. Pastures and other fields provided most of the produce farm families consumed and sold, and kept neighbors of other religions and political views out of earshot, far enough away to be easily tolerated in the casual rural way so evident in the sorts of freedoms the Constitution guarantees. And the meadow meant security in wintertime, when great piles of hay fed livestock through the dark, cold days. Well-tended meadows and cropland and barns and fences, too, advertised the thriftiness, indeed the morality, of farm families everywhere.

Wherever the explorer probes away from central cities, he or she sees domestic lawns distancing houses from streets and roads, shouting the traditional American notion that a farmhouse and barn ought to stand not grouped with others in some picturesque village but in the countryside, smack in the center of fields. Long after 1900, when for the first time a majority of Americans lived away from family farms, the lawn symbolized a devotion to a way of life left behind by people moving to towns and villages and cities, and working in factories and offices. Even after 1950, when many farm families specialized in crops and livestock that required no meadows at all, suburban Americans prized lawns because they allowed precious sunlight to bathe an entire house, the light that once gave life to crops growing around a house and barn.

Having light and wind strike all four sides of a house remains peculiarly American. While European peasants often gathered in villages where houses and sheds shared common walls, and while South American colonists built houses abutting village streets and focused outdoor activities rearward on courtyards surrounded by eight-foot-high walls, American colonists and pioneers anxious to live in the middle of their hard-won investment chose to live surrounded by open fields.

Partly the predilection originated in military necessity. Open fields were free of obstructions and allowed defenders free range to fire muskets against interlopers, and provided invaders and marauders, especially French and Indian attackers, no more place to hide during advances than cloverleaf clusters offer cover to car thieves. But mostly the predilection began in the simple realities of scale. European peasants might work five or ten acres of land within a half-hour walk from the village, but Americans, almost from the beginning, farmed much larger parcels and refused to spend a half hour, let alone an hour, walking back and forth from fields. Their determination to avoid commuting produced an early landscape Europeans called "the open-country neighborhood," the landscape the explorer examines halfway across Iowa, where houses sit in the middle of 640-acre lots, in the center of whole square miles.

And by the 1830s, that determination to live in structures surrounded by open lawns that invite light and air—while politely defending against pedestrians and giving elbow room to neighbors of different religions and customs—caused Americans to build in suburbs and commute to work. A lawn still symbolizes the moral integrity of its owner. Lawns reflect moral light.

Seven

Main Street

WHILE DISNEY CREATED EPCOT, the experimental prototypical community of tomorrow, at Disney World, real estate developers across the United States began tinkering with another sort of community, one focused, indeed fixated, on the past. In the 1970s, developers figured out that many Americans wanted to live in the stereotypical small town that Disney had stumbled onto years earlier in Disneyland, the gentle, human-scale, main-street-focused place in which people behaved themselves and automobiles seemed less than necessary. Bound up in nostalgic visual images on calendars and postcards, on syrupy 1960s television shows like *Mayberry RFD* and *Green Acres* and *Petticoat Junction,* on the jackets of long-ago best-sellers by Sinclair Lewis and recent triumphs by John Cheever, perhaps most important on the covers of hundreds of children's and young-adult novels proffered by well-meaning librarians and schoolteachers after the 1960s, books like Ray Bradbury's *Something Wicked This Way Comes,* nostalgia for the small town of fiction began driving the cosmetic makeover of small towns, at least of small-town shopping streets, everywhere in the country, and in time led to the creation of residential enclaves planned to look like something from some near-fictional past.

Stripping off vinyl and aluminum siding, replacing plate glass with mullion windows, and above all cleaning and repointing brick facades struck small-town chambers of commerce as the classy way to reinvigorate main-street retailing in an era just after the interstate evisceration of urban downtowns. Stunned by the new discount stores sparkling amid the acres of free parking created along nearby bypasses, store owners and landlords embraced the historic preservation movement as a way of getting something new and actually quite nice simply by removing the cheap facades of 1950s modernism. Somehow, they suspected, the sandblasted redbrick and ornate window and door trim reflected the timelessness, the rock-solid quality of another age. The explorer walking slowly and thoughtfully through any restored main street early Sunday morning glimpses the dates built into facades or the local historical society date-plates recently bolted on others, and marvels that whole "business blocks" and indeed entire streets seem to have been built at the same moment. Perhaps the explorer walks a bit farther, maybe over to Second Street, spots a massive, equipment-filled firehouse, and begins to think about the past that was, not the past imagined by television producers and advertising managers.

Explorers know firehouses well, for firehouses provide public rest rooms. Most small towns pour money into fire departments, and even villages usually boast handsome structures and engines paid for by nonprofit fire-department support societies. The wide overhead door, raised on all but the stormiest days, and almost always open on weekends and in the evenings, reveals pumpers and rescue trucks, ambulances and forest-fire engines, sometimes lined up three and four abreast, often two deep, every truck emblazoned with the town crest and town name. Immaculate and gleaming, the fire trucks wait, solemnly announcing that never again will Main Street burn down, as it did in 1884, 1890, 1907, or whenever it did, forcing its owners to rebuild, and to rebuild in brick.

Any exploring bicyclist riding from town to town,

perhaps pedaling a *century*—a hundred-mile trip consuming a dawn-to-dusk summer Saturday—senses that cosmetic makeover masks the long-burned but never-forgotten wooden main-street fabrics of the last century. Small-town explorers move always into the murk of fire insurance protocol, mortgage systems, all the intricacies of finance that gird the building of anything. But the main-street world re-created so lovingly by Disney, then by small-town chambers of commerce caught up in 1960s and 1970s historic preservation, perhaps best reflects the stunning power of fire insurance companies to shape building.

In the middle of the nineteenth century, fire insurance firms worried that street trees might communicate fire, especially in autumn. One chimney fire spitting sparks might torch a tree, and then the wind might shower adjacent roofs with flaming leaves as tree after tree exploded. So went the worry, and so ran the insurance policies mandating cancellation of coverage or increased premiums if owners or municipal government planted street trees. Until well into the nineteenth century (and certainly long before the age of electric lines), villages lacked street trees not because villagers lacked aesthetic awareness but simply because they lacked the tax base to purchase hand-drawn and hand-operated, then horse-drawn, steam-driven fire-fighting engines. For as long as villagers relied on bucket brigades, fire insurance companies demanded all sorts of environmental fire-prevention efforts, among them tin roofs and no street trees.

But in larger towns able to afford fire engines, fire insurance companies allowed the planting of street trees, especially if commercial structures stood built in brick. The contemporary explorer walking or biking past signs boasting that a small town has joined the list of "Tree Cities USA" for its planting and care of street trees knows that the town also boasts a splendid firehouse filled with gleaming equipment, all of which is enumerated by insurance companies classifying municipalities, then setting premiums on individual properties. The links between street trees and fire engines, so old that townspeople often know nothing of them, endure as powerfully and grimly as the ranking of fire departments according to manpower, equipment, and training programs, the ranking that determines homeowner fire insurance premium rates as ruthlessly as does the location of every structure from the nearest hydrant.

But fire engines notwithstanding, main streets burned by the dozen in the late nineteenth century in a nationwide way historians are just now beginning to study. Maybe some careless storekeeper neglected to put out his cat some night. For decades, farmers' almanacs and householders' guides warned cat owners to keep cats outdoors, especially on winter nights, lest the feline craving for warmth lead to cats afire, racing through houses and stores "communicating fire everywhere." But more likely, some wood-burning stove flared up, started a chimney fire hot enough to crumble mortar and bricks, and provided townspeople with disaster and opportunity. When Main Street burned down, it meant momentary prosperity for Second Street or Railroad Street or whatever street paralleled or intersected the chief retail and office street of a town and became for a year or so the location of businesses in temporary quarters. Even more important, it meant a clean slate on one or both sides of the retail and social armature of a town.

Nowadays small-town main streets often look so seamlessly beautiful, so evenly textured, simply because they rose rebuilt in brick or sandstone at the same moment, redone by property owners not only sharing social and aesthetic values but sharing insurance company payoff checks that bankrolled at least the first floor or the facade of a dozen new buildings. What the explorer sees with eyes momentarily closed and imagination spinning is the spectacle of late-nineteenth-century people shopping in an all-new place on a street lined with brand-new buildings, each erected in the latest style, and each erected with due regard for the buildings on either side. Almost never does the explorer find an outstanding building along any postconflagration small-town main street, but almost never does she or he discover one especially ugly either. What rewards the explorer strolling three or four times along most main streets is not the display of structures erected at the same time but the continuity of facade created by property owners and architects determined to make both sides of a retail and office street reflect and support common values.

Somehow, the explorer muses, the same spirit informs the contemporary building of planned residential enclaves. Maybe residents of the new enclaves buy a sort of nostalgia blended of safety and stability, seeking in well-built houses and condominiums something of the solidity of Main Street after the fire. Do brick buildings whisper of safety from fire after all this time? Do they somehow shape national memory still?

Now and again the bicyclist pauses along Main Street and buys an ice-cold can of Coca-Cola. How many other products endure essentially unchanged from the late 1880s? The explorer who sits on a wood-and-cast-iron bench and sips a Coca-Cola glances down at the can shimmering with condensation and ponders the issue, and ponders too the name of the soft drink Coca-Cola Classic. What is classic now in the whole built environment, now at the turn of the millennium? The light that reflects from the moist can is not the light that danced eight decades ago from the ribbed, green-glass bottle, but somehow it illuminates the longevity of some things in a time of newness triumphant. Someone, the explorer realizes, sat on the bench in 1929 and drank a Coca-Cola and wondered what the stock-market news might mean. Someone sat on the bench in 1942 and wondered if Britain would last until American forces arrived. And someone sat on the bench and watched the facade of modernism, of the International Style, ripped from the storefronts in the late 1960s. Is the taste of Coca-Cola the taste of momentary respite from activity, the taste that makes explorers realize the need for a break, for a time to think about exploring?

THE SMALL TOWN endures as the national attic of American social and spatial consciousness, a sort of frame through which further vistas are invariably viewed and twisted to fit. Always the small town is *out there*, somewhere in the Midwest, the western South, the upper Mississippi Basin, northern New England, the Pacific Northwest, the upper High Plains, and always the disenchanted city dweller or suburbanite can drive there, get out, not lock the car, somehow be home. Given the staggering bias toward small-town living implicit in public and private school reading books from kindergarten onward, it is no wonder that big-city adults understand, albeit vaguely, something about small-town way of life and small-town space.

The small town—essentially a group of stores and offices set around the main street armature, a second group of businesses, chiefly wholesale and light manufacturing and repairing, focused on a parallel street, and then the houses lining a dozen or so residential streets merging into farmland—is quintessentially childhood space. Even at midday, automobile traffic moves slowly, almost sedately, so children can move quickly, safely, sometimes running from late twentieth century into a past so remote it aches, as when a rare grade school still adjourns for lunch, and at least some children sprint home for hot soup. After school and all summer, children run errands for parents, running down to the supermarket, biking over to the farm-supply store, visiting and chatting and forgetting and hurrying in a sort of haphazard way now and then recovered by moviemakers somehow certain that the small town in 1890 was the best of all possible worlds for children if not for factory workers unemployed following the Panic.

In the 1960s, enough shopping mall developers

and designers understood small-town space and walking habits that they tried to mimic them—and failed. Even today, few malls contain so-called male-dominated stores, especially hardware stores and auto-parts stores. Mall developers tried in the 1970s to arrange stores in zigzag patterns, hoping to put a men's clothing store immediately across the concourse from one selling women's clothes, then put two gender-neutral stores—say, a greeting card and a photography store—across from each other, then another pair of gender-separated stores, but quickly learned that mall rents excluded all sorts of male-focused stores.

By the 1980s, especially as established malls lost and gained stores by attrition and so could not control the placement of stores along concourses, mall owners realized with mounting horror that attrition sometimes placed a few male-oriented stores all at one end of a mall and left the remainder of the mall filled with stores aimed only at women. No longer could they even hope that husbands and wives, girlfriends and boyfriends might promenade together, shop hand in hand, and above all spend money together. Instead they watched men congregate at nodes created by accidental location and relocation of a handful of stores, perhaps an electronics store, a hobby shop, a music store, more recently a computer game/software store. And they discovered in late 1980s recession surveys that people went to malls not always to buy but for free recreation and entertainment, that the mall had become ever more like the small town, that increasingly couples fight in the cars out in the parking lot, that men no longer like malls, that men are far more likely to visit stores not in malls, say Wal-Mart and Home Depot and gigantic bookstores sitting alone in immense parking lots.

The explorer figures out, slowly, maybe sipping an ice-cold Coca-Cola Classic, maybe eating vanilla ice cream, how the small-town Main Street still works. The explorer understands how much of it still depends on things Americans so rarely discuss, things like parking.

TYPICALLY, MAIN STREET is wide not only because its founders envisioned it as a sort of boulevard, another Broad Street or Broadway, but because width makes for lots of light and air and fire retardation, and above all, width lets people admire buildings, especially three-story buildings, from a better vantage point than narrowness. But by 1915 or so, the width of so many small-town main streets provided something else, something for which no one planned but something that proved to have immediate value. The wide main street let motorists angle park.

Angle parking remains a small-town main-street

attribute rarely recognized as something motorists and merchants find utterly delicious. The motorist pulls easily into the angled space and shuts off his or her engine while looking into a store window, perhaps not the window of the store that prompted the visit to Main Street, but certainly a window stocked with items that might attract a visit, even a purchase. And the motorist leaves almost equally effortlessly, and with a bit of panache, backing into the wide street, head craned to see oncoming cars. The backing car not only slows, then blocks traffic, causing stopped motorists to glance around at store windows, but the potential for encountering backing cars makes all motorists slow down and drive warily. Even the cruising bicyclist slows and watches carefully for any rearward movement, any brake lights or back-up lights.

Decades ago, angle parking struck men as women-friendly. By the 1930s, as cars grew heavy and long but well before the advent of inexpensive power steering, women learned what men knew: Parallel parking demanded not only skill and strength but the attention and goodwill of the motorist behind, the motorist who had to stop short, and perhaps even back up, while the parking motorist maneuvered backward into a space that might prove too short. Tall women, like tall men, parallel parked best, partly because when reversing they could see farther to the right, but largely because they could brace them-selves against floorboards and turn the large wheels that levered big-wheeled, awesomely stiff front ends. Trained drivers knew parallel parking was merely a trick: Given parked cars all of the same length, one merely pulls one's front wheels parallel to the front wheels of the car parked in front of the empty space, turns the steering wheel fully to the right, reverses until one's front wheels are parallel to the rear wheels of the car in front of the space, then spins the steer-ing wheel all the way to the left, then backs almost to the front bumper of the car behind the space.

The trick worked into the middle 1960s, when motorists discovered the new geometrics of parallel parking behind a Volkswagen, then behind the flood of tiny cars from Asia. By the late 1960s, the combina-tion of shopping-mall and commercial-strip parking lots and the widely disparate lengths of automobiles drove many hitherto accurate parallel parkers to dis-traction, even after they bought cars equipped with power steering. No longer made to practice parallel parking routinely, and faced with short cars that wrecked techniques, parallel parkers lost their skills and lost the ability to teach teenagers. Twenty years later, many states eliminated the parallel parking re-quirement from driver's license examinations. Too many teenagers flunked.

Angle parking endures, then, as a small-town

bonus, but usually only along Main Street. On Second Street and the other less important commercial streets, customers expect to parallel park or pull into small lots, many still unpaved, built on the sites of long-demolished buildings. Merchants pay higher rent for Main Street locations, although often not nearly the rents paid for shopping mall space, in large part because angle parking makes Main Street work for the errand-running shopper, the woman driving into town to buy a greeting card, the man stopping for a haircut, the teenagers pulling in for ice cream. Quick in, quick out, what so many shoppers want when they want it. But then, angle parking, simply because it slows through traffic, subtly shifts it onto some parallel street, which often does at least a few merchants some good.

Only along Main Street does window shopping from cars remind the explorer that woman-driver jokes originated long after the introduction of the flivver and never gained much currency in cities too jammed with traffic to permit, let alone reward, window shopping. The woman driver of so many low-life comedian jokes originated in small towns, when women simply stopped on Main Street to glance at a sign screaming "sale" or slowed to study a new window display. Most small-town women understood simply that Main Street existed largely for them, and that they controlled behavior along it. Men fumed, swore at slow-moving cars drifting slightly to the right or left, then shook heads in astonishment at impromptu, unsignaled turns into angled spaces. Only rarely did they admit among themselves that the small-town women drivers almost never hit anything and had accident rates far lower than those of the men who prided themselves on never looking right or left, at zooming along meandering roads lined with utility poles, at racing mail trains to grade crossings.

Angle-parking and slow-moving, eye-wandering women drivers made Main Street safe for roaming children, and dogs, even bicyclists, who discover when they ride from exurbs into rural countryside that however dangerous backing cars might be, they represent less of a danger than parallel-parked driver doors flung open in their path. The planners and developers of American *joka-machi* struggle with fences and buffer zones and speed bumps to accomplish something that small towns provided in the horse-drawn age and still provide today: a safe place for kids. And however much small-town kids may pine for the big-city excitement they see on television, few of them want to live behind the fences of planned residential developments. Who wants to live where one has to ask Mom to drive all the way to the comic-book store? Why not bicycle to the comic-book store, leave one's bike unlocked on the sidewalk, and spend an hour inside among one's friends?

Small-town children know what the explorer discovers only after much scrutiny. Small-town retail space today shelters a rich mix of commercial operations that make shopping mall concourses extraordinarily dull. Some proportion of the diversity originates in the murk of fire insurance policies and commercial leases. Many shopping mall proprietors simply prohibit merchants from selling any flammable liquids at all, and many others forbid the sale of any secondhand merchandise. The would-be hardware store owner discovers that prohibitions against selling kerosene and refilling propane tanks automatically deflect would-be buyers of lanterns and gas grills, and the would-be hobby shop owner realizes that regulations against selling everything from tenth-hand Lionel trains to secondhand comic books and Magic Cards eliminate profitable lines of business. So Main Street fills not with marginal businesses but with businesses that either cannot or will not afford shopping mall rents or shopping mall restrictions. Even stodgy chambers of commerce slowly realize that given a healthy mix of such main-street businesses, new shopping malls or discount stores represent very little threat indeed.

The explorer discovers reassuring realities. Wal-

Mart sells no marine paint, but the Main Street paint store still furnishes paint to yachtsmen fitting out in April. Home Depot sells no beekeeping supplies, but the Main Street hardware store still furnishes supers, foundation, and hive tools in the back room, adjacent to canning supplies, a few aisles away from harness-repair tools needed by little girls owning their first ponies. The music store at the shopping mall sells a few electric guitars, but the Main Street music store displays, sells, and delivers used acoustic guitars, electric guitars, even pianos, and upstairs has a music studio complete with after-school piano teacher. Main Street stores offer the prospect of treasure finding.

Hobby shops and sporting goods stores still enliven Main Street, still compete well against both shopping mall stores and mail-order firms, even against category-buster megastores. In large part, they succeed because they buy and sell used goods, their stock turns over frequently and unexpectedly, and they have a much larger clientele than many motorists suppose. The explorer probing on Saturdays glimpses the out-of-state license plates on the cars angled parked before the stores, and stops to scrutinize. What brings customers from so far away? Inside the answers are everywhere, in cardboard boxes beneath and behind counters, on shelves lining back rooms, on goods hanging from ceilings. Always the stock is changing, and every day something old turns up. No wonder so many small-town main-street stores do such a large mail-order business, something the explorer notices in late afternoon, when the UPS man leaves the stores carrying boxes, not empty-handed.

Main Street always inveigles the bicyclist-explorer, because the bicyclist knows that bicycle stores locate in small towns where bicycling is still seen as safe and fun, and where bicycle store owners find the medium-rent locations that reward the buying and selling and trading of secondhand and twelfth-hand bicycles. No matter that the exploring bicyclist is well equipped with spare tube, tools, and air pump. The bicyclist, like all explorers, inspects all sources of potential help and resupply, and finds that main-street bicycle stores invariably offer a rest room to any bicyclist and to anyone else too. And like the hobby shop, the sporting goods store, the bookstore, like so many shops along the small-town main street, the bicycle store reveals the same stunning range of prices. Swaying on cables strung from the ceiling, the $3,500 Merlin awaits a buyer more rare than the proud mother inquiring after a used sidewalk bike priced around fifteen bucks. Somewhere in the back of the shop is a workbench, an air compressor, and a rack of tools, where the exploring bicyclist can get a broken spoke fixed on short notice, where young children hang around, learning how a bike gets assembled quickly, where a bike-smitten high school girl finds a job that pays better than the fast-food place on the bypass.

In the 1970s, perhaps in the energy-crisis years especially, merchants who had lost faith in Main Street and relocated to commercial-strip stores realized that the empty storefronts they left behind had begun to fill with experimental businesses, often ones owned by women. When those businesses prospered, the renegades frequently attempted to move back and discovered that Main Street had been taken over by handicraft and antique dealers, and those businesspeople, especially the women antique dealers, riding a retailing wave rarely noticed in newspapers and business journals, had begun the boutiquing of Main Street, adding greatly to its richness.

Isolated antique dealers struggle to attract customers. A cluster of antique shops along Main Street enables a group of dealers to prosper as components of a larger whole, while giving each proprietor the freedom of a self-contained storefront. No special overhead or operating regulations plague the group or its individual members, and the stores offer almost perfect spaces. Large windows and high ceilings let antique dealers stack merchandise, and cellars and second floors provide inexpensive, on-site storage. The alley behind the Main Street business blocks offers direct access to the rear of the store, and the explorer quickly discovers as much activity behind the stores as on the sidewalks and steps in front. Unlike the metal-shrouded mall, Main Street offers a retailer two entranceways, one for buyers and one for sellers, and moreover enables buyers to move bulky items through the rear of the store directly into cars and pickup trucks. Once free of using the front entrance as shipping portal too, antique dealers immediately dress up their front windows and doors and doorsteps, sometimes spilling their goods onto sidewalks and giving Main Street the long-lost festive air of 1950s midsummer sidewalk sales.

A few antique shops newly located on Main Street are enough to begin attracting the antiquing crowd, the immense cohort of Americans fascinated with old things and very often willing to pay high sums for them, perhaps to furnish their homes in residential enclaves. Wherever antique shops blossom along Main Street, wherever the antique dealers hang out flags, repaint facades, and set ancient sleds and chairs on the sidewalk, there the explorer knows that good restaurants have also opened. Art galleries and bookshops, especially secondhand bookshops, follow the arrival of antique stores and one or two new restaurants. Like the antique dealers, the art gallery owners prize the large windows and high ceilings of the old stores, but perhaps their understanding that certain types of paintings sell well to people already owning ornate frames does as much to encourage their relocation to small towns. Booksellers value the large stores and high ceilings too, of course, but they know that antique collectors not only read but are likely to read old books, and sometimes are looking to buy sets of great authors to make their newly acquired golden-oak bookcases look right.

In the middle 1980s, antique dealer associations had begun distributing maps showing the location of antique-dealer clusters, but at the end of the 1990s, the explorer finds the brochures in state-line tourist-information kiosks touting scenic tours not only for antique collectors but for buyers of new paintings and used books. Always the brochures direct motorists, and determined bicyclists, toward a route punctuated with renovated main streets.

A sort of clerisy now shops away from the commercial strips and regional malls and factory outlet clusters that at first glance seem to draw all the retail business of the country. The clerisy has time to shop, often devoting a weekend to a leisurely shopping trip miles from home. It is a group as yet unmarked by news media dependent on shopping mall advertising, but it assuredly threatens the owners of upscale shopping malls already worried that many two-income couples buy most of their clothing from mail-order firms and are bored beyond measure with mall shopping. Retail analysts know what the explorer knows. In the boutiqued main-street shops, the stock is wholly unpredictable and continuously changing, not only enticing the young couple furnishing a first condo, but inveigling the retired couple intrigued with collecting period signboards. A good antique shop, a good secondhand bookstore, offers variety and serendipitous experience—or at least the *chance* of a serendipitous experience—no mall can begin to match. And a first-rate Main Street pulsing with specialized shops becomes a place a family, even a family with young teenagers, can visit happily.

Walking or pedaling very slowly through the crowds on a weekend main street, or stopped eating ice cream, leaning against a brick wall warm in the sun, the explorer looks above storefront level and sees the signs of old fraternal orders, whose meeting rooms cover entire second stories of small-town buildings. International Order of Odd Fellows, the Red Men, the Benevolent and Fraternal Order of Elks, the Masons—all more or less descend from the mid-nineteenth-century loneliness and anxiety of small-town men traveling on business and anxious for some sort of brotherhood support in towns and cities far from home. To be sure, the older orders and the newer ones like the Kiwanis and Rotary and Lions exist mostly to do good, the Masons raising thousands of dollars a day nationwide to operate fee-free hospitals for burned and crippled children, the Rotary giving scholarships for foreign travel and study, the Lions funding vision research and testing. But they still speak strongest to small-town men searching for some sort of fellowship beyond the satellite dish, some focus on something better than everyday money-getting perhaps.

For all that urban people see them as hokey, and for all that urban people know almost nothing about them anyway, the explorer trying to realize—to *make real*—a small town sees the metal signs with the cryptic logos and knows that fraternal orders still matter to small-town men. How they matter, the explorer cannot quite decide, but the signs ranged outside towns, the signs sometimes clustered on a metal frame adjacent to secondary highways, almost always have smaller signs beneath explaining that the Masons meet every third Thursday evening at 7:00 P.M. in the Masonic Hall, that the Kiwanis chapter meets every third Wednesday for lunch at a restaurant on the bypass. And the signs are rarely rusted, never vandalized, almost invariably glistening in their porce-lain-enamel finish. They speak to the explorer of a web of small-town connections reaching from Maine to California, a web not on-line. They speak of in-stantaneous acceptance, of an immediate meal, prob-ably free, for members, of men still intrigued in civic duty, charity, morality-based self-improvement ef-forts.

The explorer stopped to rest on Main Street or a few miles away by the metal frame carrying the fra-ternal-order signs aimed at motorists approaching Main Street sees something else, the overhead wires that hint at fiber-optic connections, the miniature satellite dishes that suggest that small-town busi-nesses are linking up electronically, that the bypass businesses may be bypassed soon.

Often the fraternal-order signs announce lunch at a Holiday Inn, Best Western, or other motel res-taurant out on the bypass circling around Main Street, around the whole town. The bicyclist-explorer riding long back-road distances, from one small town to another to another, discovers in the pattern of edge-of-town fraternal-order signs something of the lingering rents in small-town, main-street fabric. Most small towns offer no room for the night, at least not near Main Street, not even a bed-and-breakfast in a big, well-porched house a block or so away on

Maple Street. At best they offer a sign announcing a Comfort Inn or Days Inn a few miles away, a sign sometimes decorated with fraternal-order signs implying that while Main Street might have a good diner or even a decent restaurant, it lacks any place where thirty-five or sixty Kiwanians or Rotarians can sit down, eat, and discuss the next charitable effort. Small towns still put up most visitors in homes, for the old hotel abandoned above its ground floor, or long converted to elderly housing, has accepted no guests since the demise of railroad passenger-train service in the 1950s. The explorer can visit Main Street, but almost never can the explorer stay overnight. Always he or she must walk or ride away from town, through the woods or fields, toward the main-traveled road, toward the highway, toward the interstate highway, toward the motel.

Eight

Stops

MOTELS STAND WHERE they do across rural America, across most of metropolitan America in fact, because motel siting experts prefer large lots of cheap land near well-traveled highways, preferably adjacent to interstate highway off-ramps. The experts choose sites according to complex formulas built around the long-distance automobile traveler driving the speed limit hour after hour. Eight hours from a major metropolitan area is a good general site for a motel, for by then most motorists are tired, anxious for a hot meal, a sparkling pool, a decent bed. Within the general location, the experts seek an interstate highway interchange with a well-traveled state highway, especially a highway offering a direct route between two small cities, or between a metropolitan region and a recreational area, perhaps a national park or national forest. And always the experts try to locate a few acres for the motel site, even part of a farm on the near side of the exit, so anxious motorists can see the motel before they see the actual exit ramp, and so know that the motel is immediately accessible. Large signs along the interstate highway announce the presence of a Holiday Inn or Best Western thirty or seven or two miles ahead, but the actual building is the best proof that it exists, and that the motorist need not wander far along secondary roads to find it.

Motels get little attention from weary motorists anxious to pull in for the night, shower, walk around a bit, eat, maybe have a beer in the bar, then shower again and fall into bed. Maybe the room interior gets a bit of attention of the where-did-they-get-these-fake-paintings sort, and sometimes the shower faucets demand sustained analysis in pursuit of hot water. The building itself, so often seen momentarily at end of day, in fatigue, then briefly glimpsed in the morning through the rearview mirror, acquires no scrutiny from architectural historians, but the explorer realizes that motel-zone activity rewards a bit of study. Motels serve more than lunching Rotarians and coast-to-coast vacationers, salesmen, and college students heading to and from bachelor-degree education.

At night they anchor nightlife. At least on Friday and Saturday night, cloverleaf motels offer miniature nightclubs that attract the swinging social set of entire rural counties, sometimes hundreds of couples, enough to justify not just a guitar or piano player but a whole five-person band. Something must happen beyond the ordinary accommodation of guests to justify the immense parking lots, the explorer muses, walking or pedaling in a widening gyre around the blacktop surface more or less in front of the motel, surrounding its portico and offering parking for two hundred or more cars away from the rooms.

Of course, entertainment happens in the daylight hours too, especially when wedding receptions are held in the nightclub–become–banquet room for the afternoon, or when the Kiwanis Club invites two other clubs to a massive luncheon to discuss a stunningly expensive, regional-scale charity project. And, the explorer discovers wholly accidentally, all day on Saturday some motels host special events that fill the parking lot and banquet room both: a Christmastime craft fair, a special gathering of rare-book dealers, a gun show and sale, the regionwide Barbie-doll collectors' semiannual sale and swap meet, the statewide baseball-card show.

At night, the parking lot thronged with cars makes clear the limitations of the dark and deserted

Main Street two miles away, the small town with sidewalks rolled for the night, the small town lacking a motel, the small town with a gasoline station closed at dusk, the main street cloaked in quiet dark. Out on the bypass, out by the interstate highway, the motel owns the night, its many lights shining down over both its parking lots, its handful of old-fashioned outdoor post and wall lanterns sparkling by its main entrance, its dozens or hundreds of smaller, single-bulb lights flicked on, one beside each room door. It is the Admiral Benbow, the Jamaica Inn, the inn of old, the low-slung, thatched-roof, stone-built inn of countless European folktales and juvenile adventure stories and gothic romances, the two-story, wood-frame inn of the country's colonial past, the only building lit through the colonial night, its one candle glimmering against the black, summoning and welcoming the benighted, bewildered traveler.

Only rarely does the contemporary traveler probe the back lot of the motel, the zone fenced off with chain-link fencing laced with strips of somber-hued, opaque plastic or screened with tall-growing junipers well fertilized and never pruned, the place that the explorer finds so intriguing. In the back lot, the explorer finds the parking area for the employee cars, and from the cars he or she knows that motel employment makes no one rich. The cars cluster around the loading dock that every morning sees deliveries of food and on Saturday nights sees aspiring musicians struggling with electric guitars, amplifiers, mixers, and immense speakers, all meticulously and lovingly off-loaded from battered pickup trucks. In the back lot, the air is scented with the detergent in which sheets and pillowcases and towels are washed, and sometimes too the explorer pacing the far fringes of motel domain scents the odor of overwhelmed septic systems buried in the seemingly vacant lot beyond the manicured parking area. Usually the Dumpster smells a bit too, but since motels expect guests to use air-conditioning, to avoid ever opening windows, the odors of septic system field and Dumpster find their way to other noses, toward the mobile homes and tiny houses that often abut motel back lots, the residential zones linked to motel parking lots by the dirt trails the explorer instantly recognizes and sometimes follows.

By day, the motel is oasis, especially for children. Smaller motels provide only outdoor pools useful in summertime, but since the 1970s energy crisis most respectable chain motels provide an indoor pool, usually one located some distance from the banquet room–nightclub zone frequented by locals.

Surrounded on two or more sides by glass, often roofed with glass, the indoor pool becomes substitute hearth for adults not particularly anxious to meet strangers but willing to engage in casual conversation scented by chlorine. Outdoor or indoor, the pool focuses the motel children, who immediately discover and rediscover the way the pool offers instantaneous release from the behavioral restrictions imposed by long auto trips. Like the fireplace of ancient inns, the pool gathers in strangers, and strangers begin to talk. Water loosens the spirit, relaxes, somehow loosens the mantle of reserve with which traveling Americans now clothe themselves, and provides a smidgen of the Bahamas, Grenada, Aruba next to asphalt.

No piece of America is more typical than the clump of businesses by the cloverleaf, isolated from everything else. Two or three motels, one or two gasoline stations, perhaps one or two fast-food places, and maybe a short-order chain restaurant, such is the typical cluster. Why spend a day just walking or bicycling around the businesses straddling the interstate, exploring casually? Why not learn to study something about which no books yet exist, and which reveals much about the built environment?

No fences, no gates, no guards keep trespassers from the enclave intended to serve travelers, but the cluster of businesses is every bit as much an enclave as the new residential developments sprouting everywhere in outer suburban regions. The cluster seems so patently, so insistently porous that travelers understand it only as something through which everyone passes, either staying on the interstate highway or exiting for a few minutes to fuel, for five minutes to use rest rooms and buy hamburgers-to-go, maybe for a night in a room one cannot remember a week later. But the explorer moving beyond the motel back lot knows instantly that people work day after day in the cluster surrounded by woods and agricultural fields, that the high-speed cross of interstate highway and secondary road pulses with a life of its own, an intent of its own.

Everything built in the cluster exists only in the short-term thinking of retail marketing. No structure stands facing the ages, and few stand facing more than a decade or two. Gasoline stations, motels, fast-food restaurants all glisten in chrome, glass, stucco, and plastic, but none is intended to endure. And none is intended to age gracefully.

The explorer wheeling behind the motel, around the gasoline station, between the taco and pizza restaurants sees everywhere not just the signs of continuous, casual maintenance, say the pails and mops and squeegees devoted to gleaming entrance foyers and plate-glass windows, but the evidence of continual repair and restoration. Almost every cluster boasts a structure being *fixed*, somehow stayed again against deterioration. A plumber's truck stands parked behind the restaurant, a ladder leans against the back of the gas station, a pile of drainpipe and a ditching machine snuggle against the motel Dumpster. Often the repair seems utterly cosmetic, new paint being applied, all the parking lot lights being replaced on the same day, a new sign being nudged onto a concrete pad bristling with electric conduit. Sometimes the explorer spies accessories undergoing face-lifts or replacement, the soft-drink vending machine getting a new facade or being dragged toward a truck equipped with lowered hydraulic tailgate. At night or at daybreak, the explorer discovers the paint-spattered truck and paint-spattered men spraying new lines on parking lots, and always the explorer sees the landscapers, the men and women servicing shrubbery, making pets of plants.

No place in the country better exemplifies the changing attitude toward plants. Everywhere in the interchange cluster, the explorer walks or pedals past a stunning uniformity of plants, a short list of species developed by landscape architects and project engineers and useful at any building site almost anywhere in the nation. Set down in narrow beds bordering parking lots and usually edging the facades of restaurants and motels, the short-list plants demonstrate a subtle but near-fanatic allegiance to dwarf evergreens. Dwarf junipers and yews edge almost every new commercial structure in the United States. Trees are peculiarly absent from most cluster landscapes, although now and then a hedge of high-growing juniper shields the far end of the parking lot from the grassy shoulder of the interstate highway just beyond, and a hybrid maple or two sits in a huge ring of wood chips. What explains the absence of trees, especially of pines and spruce whose evergreen characteristics might complement the evergreen yews?

Everywhere in the cluster, designers create open views, long vistas that not only encourage motorists to look ahead, but provide no places where a moving automobile might be shielded by plants from an oncoming motorist. But far more important is the determined effort to remove—or, to speak more accurately, to never plant—any vegetation that will screen a criminal. Everywhere the explorer stares, the explorer sees long distances uninterrupted by tall-growing plants.

Plants become pets everywhere in the clusters, and not especially beloved pets. They are "installed" just before the business opens, usually planted quite near together to make beds look mature from the beginning, which is the first reason designers choose dwarf species. Ordinary species grow, get bushy, touch each other, and *demand pruning*. The dwarf species remain almost as installed, demand little in the way of pruning, and never grow tall enough to mask a crouching villain. Moreover, dwarf species make bark mulch look good, simply because they never spread their branches so far that mulch vanishes completely from view. Everywhere in the cluster, dwarf plants grow above bark mulch routinely reapplied over a base layer of plastic. The mulch, so obviously new-laid, reassures customers that they walk across a clean, cared-for site, but more important for the business owners, the mulch masks the plastic sheets that inhibit weed growth.

Weeds are few in most clusters, not because landscapers regularly remove them but because they have no habitat. Weeds are like dirt, and dirt belongs nowhere in the motel–restaurant–gas station cluster, because decades ago analysts of retail sales discovered Americans loathe dirty rest rooms, messy gasoline stations, and crummy motels. If an American motorist is expected to get out of his or her automobile and buy anything, especially gasoline he or she pumps, dirt must be eradicated, and everything that resembles dirt, connotes dirt, springs from dirt.

So the dwarf plants become petlike, cared for not as wild things, almost not as domestic creatures, but essentially as housebroken pets, trusted to never misbehave, to never drop leaves that might resemble wastepaper litter, to never grow and never get sick. The short list of plants makes the replacement of a dying or dead plant easy, cheap, and fast, ensuring a permanent, homogeneous border or clump of green above bark-mulch brown.

The explorer looking from one gasoline station to another or walking from one fast-food franchise to the next suddenly realizes that the dwarf plants are only one component in a larger marketing strategy. Every interstate highway interchange provides services and products almost immediately consumed, hamburgers, a bed for the night, a tank of gasoline. So in order to create the permanent memories that shape repeat sales, a decades-old advertising gimmick has become an industry itself. Interchange businesses give away trinkets. Children eating hamburgers play with plastic figures representing characters in the latest animated film, and adults buying soft drinks get reusable plastic mugs contoured to fit in automobile consoles. Customers get plastic litter bags or insulated sandwich boxes or a dozen other gimmicks intended to remind them to stop again in the way free drinking glasses long ago reminded travelers to fill up at particular gasoline stations. All the gimmicks reflect an almost pathetic worry by merchandisers that the interchange experience is so ordinary and so momentary that automobilists retain no specific memories, not even product loyalty.

Around the motel, along the frontage road, across the bridge arching about the interstate highway, the explorer discovers not so much the complexity of the ordinary interstate highway interchange but the ease with which most people dismiss both interchange space and interchange experience. Can places become so ordinary that they become invisible? Is it possible for motorists to forget whole chunks of their drive, to be unable to recall at which interchange they bought gas or stopped for a cold drink? What exactly makes interchanges so peculiarly forgettable, so exquisitely unseeable? The explorer who stops early at a motel and spends an hour or so walking around not only stretches muscles but stretches concepts of place. An interchange is not a village, not a station, not something with its own zip code. It is a place to park, to get out and walk and look, to see a piece of landscape wrenched from tradition and somehow insinuating that well-kept places are the easiest to forget.

And at midmorning, when the explorer glances about at the motels and realizes that all are empty of guests, the explorer begins discovering the limitations of language.

Is a motel at midday a vacant motel?

VACANCY ITSELF IS an obscure concept nowadays, one brought to mind by brightly lit "no vacancy" motel signs or word-of-mouth knowledge of an apartment or house for rent. But never does a motel sign read "part empty." Vacancy is a concept like guilt, its nuances suggested when a jury finds a defendant not innocent but "not guilty." Why does a defendant plead "guilt or not guilty" rather than "guilty or innocent"? Is an abandoned, derelict motel a vacant one? Is a lot occupied by wild plants and animals vacant only because people now presume a lot exists for a structure?

Fields are not vacant lots. A field filled with maturing pumpkin plants is a for-profit place, one fenced and fertilized and weeded, one reflecting continuous enterprise. After harvest, the field is empty of pumpkins and vines but is scarcely vacant. Even when a field is abandoned, even when the first pioneer plants invade its soil, no one thinks of it as vacant. Maybe a few elderly people remember the expression "old field" and apply it to the abandoned acreage, but most passersby note the wild grasses, shrug, and call the field a field. A field big enough for crop raising or for livestock grazing is too big to be a lot, and whatever its condition, it cannot be vacant.

Any explorer trying to differentiate between a field and a lot quickly discovers something of the antiquity and complexity of landscape terminology. Attorneys still call large pieces of land by old terms indeed, referring glibly to *tracts* or *parcels* of land, territory, space, and understand that such large pieces can be *subdivided*. Of course, the explorer realizes when passing a farm, a condominium cluster under construction, even a vacant lot, any piece of land can be subdivided. But gradually the explorer of ordinary landscape realizes how deeply the laws of real-property ownership affect legal terminology and ordinary language too. A parcel of land can be divided, but the law presumes the smaller divisions are themselves profitable, traditionally as farms or farm fields, more lately as pieces of land that can be divided into lots, into house lots. And while house lots can be divided, as when two abutting landowners decide to split the vacant lot between their own, ordinarily they are not, since local ordinances restrict the size of house lots. A lot, then, is typically the smallest *buildable* piece of land, according to local ordinances.

Ordinarily, ordinances express lot size in acres or fractions of acres. Across most of the country, half-acre lots are common, but many communities mandate one-acre lots, and many others prohibit building houses on lots less than a quarter acre. Whatever the twentieth-century tendency toward the metric system, landowners resist the change to hectares, preferring the ancient and nowadays American-only measurements at first glance nearly impossible to understand. But explorers willing to count their paces, to look precisely at distances between houses, to gaze out across a farm field, open their minds to the longevity of landholding custom.

Land-measurement terms usually express more than mere area. An acre, for example, originated as the area one man and two oxen could plow in a day. Over the centuries, peasants averaged out length of day, strength of oxen, skill of plowmen into an understanding of area based on the length of a furrow the plowman and oxen plowed before needing to rest. A furlong, then, is a furrow long, the length team and man could strain before needing a rest. Such ancient lore, known for generations as *ground rules*, involved everything from deciding the shape of fields to laying out the foundations of a house.

Square fields require less fencing than rectangular ones, for example, but explorers quickly discover that farmers prefer rectangular fields. A square field 400 feet on a side contains 160,000 square feet and needs 1,600 feet of fence. A rectangular field 200 by 800 feet encloses the same area but must have 2,000 feet of fencing. Why, then, would a farmer choose to lay out rectangular fields? The explorer finds the answer in watching a farmer operate a tractor across a field or a homeowner run a lawn mower across a lawn. The square field demands more turnarounds than the rectangular one, and turning around wastes time and effort.

Ground rules once upon a time governed all sorts of design and building activities. A family about to build a house, even a log cabin, first set four pegs into the ground to roughly mark the four corners, then stretched a rope diagonally between them. By moving the pegs a bit until the diagonals were equal, the family created the right-angled, square shape absolutely necessary to building a structure quickly and well. No one in the family needed a measuring tape, and indeed no one needed to know arithmetic, geometry, or even how to read. The ground rules had evolved long before ordinary people knew such things, and the explorer walking past a construction site with eyes wide open sees the ground rules in use today.

In almost every new house, electric outlets are a specific distance above the floor. The distance is that of the electrician's hammer. Rather than measure, the electrician sets the hammer on end, holds the electric box against the wall, then lifts the hammer and spikes the box.

Casual measuring activity spied by any explorer walking past carpenters or bulldozer operators long ago shaped federal policy. Thomas Jefferson wanted all measurement to be decimal-based, but John Adams argued for keeping the old system. Adams charged that Jefferson's newfangled innovation aided only the rich, who prospered as their wealth multiplied. The traditional system, Adams argued, aided the ordinary citizen because it fostered easy division of wealth. So long as eggs were sold by the dozen, groups of two, three, four, six, and twelve could join together and buy a dozen eggs, but if eggs were sold by the ten, only groups of two, five, and ten could pool resources. But Adams had more critical issues in mind than dozens of eggs. He knew that every square mile of land contains 640 acres, and that on the frontier, a square mile of land could be apportioned to a single family or easily divided between two or four families. Indeed a square mile of land could be divided among sixteen families, giving each family forty acres, the minimum agriculturists thought sufficient to maintain a family—and a mule. Moreover, Adams convinced Jefferson that townships in the West ought to be surveyed in multiples of square miles, each township being six miles square and so containing thirty-six "sections" of land, each of 640 acres. In the end, the two parties compromised. Jefferson won his decimal-based currency system, and Adams won a landscape based on the ancient ground rules.

Any explorer who walks or bicycles across any rural part of the country west of the Appalachians sees the fruit of the Jefferson-Adams debate. All roads other than a few automobile-era highways and the interstate highway are straight, and cross each other at right angles, exactly a mile apart. Sometimes the explorer sees mostly the checkerboard of square or rectangular fields, but other times the explorer focuses on the gridiron of lines, the crosshatching made by straight roads, nowadays still often unpaved, crossing each other at right angles almost everywhere. A little musing makes the explorer wonder how well a grid fits onto a spherical earth, and once in a great while the explorer finds a "section correction," a place where straight roads intersect not at a right-angle crossroads but at two T intersections perhaps a hundred yards apart. A section correction tweaks the great grid back into harmony with itself, by admitting that longitude lines converge near the north pole. Now state and county highway authorities attempt to eliminate the paired intersections that surprise back-road motorists lulled by the crossroads-every-mile pattern, but the explorer who looks can still find them.

And the explorer who thinks about slang realizes how American English still includes terms like *square deal* and *square meal*, terms that originated centuries earlier in an era that prized rectilinearity. The explorer realizes that the basic landscape remains one of the Enlightenment, but enlightenment tempered by tradition apparent in miles, acres, furlongs, and by necessity in section corrections. And the explorer who glances at watch or town-hall clock grins a bit and realizes that Adams did better than Jefferson. Days still have two dozen hours and years a dozen months.

By *lot*, then, people mean something of a specific size, but something often allotted by government. From the first days of settlement onward until the official closing of the frontier in 1890, one sort of government after another allotted land to encourage pioneering, farming, ranching, mining, even railroad building. What Europeans call a *holding*, using a word that connotes something of the ancient tradition of fiefdoms, stewardship, leasing, and yeoman rights, Americans call a *lot*, using a word connoting the awarding of land sometimes in return for military service, sometimes after the payment of only a token fee. A lot of land is cousin to one's lot in life, something one almost wins, something one may do with as one chooses.

Today a lot is the smallest piece of land that supports a house, and perhaps a well and septic system too. In great cities, a lot may be a space between two row houses, a gap in a line of brick that appears like a missing tooth. In villages lacking water and sewer mains, a lot may be an acre in size but is usually rectangular, its narrow, valuable, frontage edge facing the street. Across rural regions, a lot is usually five acres, especially if subterranean water is scarce or if families tend to keep small livestock like hens.

Size and scale entertain the accomplished explorer of ordinary landscape, because they speak volumes about traditions and preferences as old as ground rules and as new as short-wheelbase cars. The explorer passes a parking lot and muses about the enduring use of the word *lot* to define places to park cars and to buy cars, especially used cars. Parking lots—what the British call *car parks*—are filled with parking spaces, what drivers in other countries call *parking places*. Space, especially seemingly empty space filled only with potential, matters intimately to Americans, who see every lot as a chance to change things, to build something new.

Every vacant lot holds cathedrals of potential. Every explorer musing about the contexts of every vacant lot imagines potentials, thinking that a lot might be a gasoline station someday or some other business. Imagining what might be built on a vacant lot begins in knowing what stands built around the lot already. Every explorer walking or bicycling begins to imagine what might be, and every explorer who returns to places over the months and years realizes how often he or she has guessed right. In every explorer pulses a bit of the real estate developer.

And in every explorer stirs a bit of the conservationist. Vacant lots reward the small-scale ecologist every bit as well as do the margins of fenced residential enclaves or disused railroad rights-of-way. Vacant lots are patches of wilderness, sometimes miniature savannas roamed by field mice and plump house cats, sometimes miniature forests sheltering nesting birds, sometimes the front porch of owls, deer, even coyote paused to look out at the manicured, built-up world of people. Lots of an acre or more are often the destination of fleeing wild animals, especially birds, and the explorer swinging along begins to realize that squirrels and birds do not move aimlessly, but with some method involving seasons or time of day. In late afternoon, for example, the explorer watches ducks and wild geese circle lower beyond the trees and houses, then disappear, and guesses that a pond lies hidden just downhill. But most wild animals head for vacant lots, and the explorer who follows them away from roadside and sidewalk finds that many of them live in burrows, that whole lots are honeycombed with tunnels.

In a vacant lot, the explorer finds underfoot not

only the ground rules that predate colonization but the cities of woodchucks and other animals that long ago made an accommodation with people and live next door. Anyone who startles a raccoon from the back porch might follow the fleeing animal just a bit and see how rapidly the chase leads to the nearest lot uncluttered with anything human.

Nine

Endings

ORDINARY AMERICAN LANDSCAPE strikes almost no one as photogenic. Here and there a historic site attracts camera-toting summer tourists, and on rare autumn occasions amateur photographers search out immense trees turning yellow and orange against blue skies. But the explorer out day after day, weekend after weekend, exploring the ordinary streets and highways and shortcuts that open on hundreds of intriguing concepts learns a little secret. Away from advertised historic sites, scenic pull-offs, and rural panoramas punctuated with traditional farmhouses and barns, anyone pointing a camera precipitates crisis, sometimes involving the high-speed arrival of police. Ordinarily police do nothing. No law prohibits photography from the roadside, and while the trespass acts forbid photography on private property, anyone may aim a camera away from the road toward private space. In upper-class residential neighborhoods already hit by burglars, in lower-class neighborhoods distrustful of any unknown authority, around factory districts routinely probed by Environmental Protection Agency officials, anywhere where insurance agents might find code violations, locals may telephone local authority, asking the police to inspect the inspectors. But fear of crime scarcely explains the harassing of photographers, usually lone photographers, pointing cameras at circling seagulls or hawks, at immense specimen sugar maples, at the last elms along a road, at the sunset blessing the church. However much walking and running and bicycling are done anonymously, the lone amateur photographer stands out, attracts unfriendly attention.

Photography threatens because photography implies notice and permanent record. Most Americans simply cannot imagine why anyone would scrutinize what they themselves ignore. Deep down, at the very core of the American psyche, they know too that they are unable to make sense of the landscape around them, that someday a stranger may come and see the jewel they missed, and after seeing it, will take it away. Yet for all they distrust their own ability to verbalize what they see and know and think about the ordinary landscape around them, they do feel for it, and in fact they seem to love it very deeply. The vacant lot, taken for granted year after year, somehow holds treasures of memory and vision, for the photographer aiming a camera at the vacant lot quickly attracts people wanting to know what the photography portends. Only in rare places does change strike abutters and neighbors as likely to be good. Ordinary landscape fits like an old shoe, comfortably, without conscious notice by its wearer, and the photographer of it threatens the change that might pinch and squeak forever after.

The explorer is dismayed at the deepening dread of casual photography, for the explorer realizes it is the by-product of deepening ignorance, the ignorance that makes asking directions stunningly revealing, sometimes perilous. Not so much lost as rambling, the explorer ten miles from home asks a man raking leaves, a woman painting a mailbox, three teenagers hanging out the simplest of questions. Where does that road go? Does that street swing back by the bridge? Is it a nice walk or ride this way to Someplace? Answers stun. However helpful, friendly, and anxious to please, the respondents admit defeat. They do not know. And beneath their ignorance not infrequently stirs a rising doubt, an uneasiness not truculent but snappish. It produces a question in return.

Why does the inquirer want to know?

Behind the question lies not so much the grudging envy of the runner or in-line skater burning calories and engaging in cardiovascular exercise the way the newspaper columnists insist all Americans should, but the dark curiosity that makes roadside photographers cringe. Why make a photograph here? Why want to ride down that road? What explains interest?—interest demanding the physical exertion of walking or pedaling, interest in places inhabitants know as neither especially beautiful nor otherwise valuable if they know them intimately at all.

Stopped, leaning against a utility pole or astride a bike leaning ever so slightly sideways, the explorer murmurs something about a nice day for a ride, about needing some exercise, about needing to be home by dark. Above the explorer and the puzzled listener, communication wires hum faintly in the breeze, adding their voice to the conversation, reminding the explorer how much they stitch together Americans with programmed messages unlike the odd, disconcerting questions the explorer asks. The walker swinging along glancing to the right and left, the bicyclist riding along *looking*, the walker or bicyclist moving around in a circle while staring at something, the explorer stopped for a minute or so to stare at some part of the seeming jumble of the built environment—

that explorer makes clear that information exists in unprogrammed ways, that the explorer commands the tools of self-directed scrutiny and discrimination. But only in the fleeting conversations with leaf rakers, mailbox checkers, newspaper getters does the explorer discover how wary Americans are now of anyone who scrutinizes the ordinary.

After a weekend or so of exploring, after looking around three or four or twenty miles from home, the explorer grasps at the magic peculiar to riding with eyes and mind open. Unlike the surging glow of the walker or bicyclist racing other walkers or bicyclists, or racing against times established a week or year before, but nonetheless akin to the rush an athlete experiences, the explorer flushes at noticing something—a tiny detail like a trace of pollution in a nearby brook, a hole roughly cut through the chain-link fence guarding the power-line substation, the smoke-smudged, fire-scorched, but seemingly useful power tools tossed in a heap behind the machine shop, an antique wooden boat nestled against a brush pile awaiting a match, the cigar box crammed with daguerreotypes atop a trash barrel perched on the curb, a Summer Help Wanted sign in the window of a brooding, ivy-covered brick structure, a piece of land graced by a long-faded real estate agency sign.

Discovery, immediate discovery, intimate discovery prompts more exploration, another ride, a slightly longer ride, more glimmers into all sorts of things: the surveyors marking out a shopping mall skeleton deep in the woods, the police officer fast asleep in his car at daybreak, the teenagers furtively disappearing downhill along a well-worn path, the nearly invisible shortcut through scrub trees and dunes to the beach, the tiny house for sale by owner at the end of a six-mile dirt road, the sudden sprouting of miniature television-reception satellite dishes everywhere in leafy suburbs bereft of children playing outdoors, the stunning sunrise view behind the auto dealership. Everything but everything is out of sequence, unprogrammed, unnoticed by everyone but the explorer exploring, glimpsing, discovering.

Discovering bits and pieces of peculiar, idiosyncratic importance in ordinary metropolitan landscape scrapes away the deep veneer of programmed learning that overlies and smothers the self-directed learning of childhood and adolescence. Making some idiosyncratic pattern of the bits and pieces shatters the veneer and enables the walker or bicyclist to navigate according to landmarks and inklings and constellations wholly personal. Abandoned commercial greenhouses, outcroppings of igneous rock, maybe first-rate and second-rate ice cream stores, whatever the concatenation of fragments become a skein into which new fragments fall into place. The exploring, discovering walker or bicyclist creates a personal whole, realizes the relations of railroad rights-of-way and telephone poles, of wholesale grocery warehouses and mom-and-pop grocery stores, of political edges versus edges of watersheds. Nothing profound, nothing earth-shattering, but everything fitting into a private worldview.

Direct contact, face-to-face with warm breezes and freezing rain, sometimes vulnerable, the explorer learns to weigh risk, to balance exertion and danger and discovery and relaxation.

Unprogrammed exercise and a rediscovery of what schools and employers and television and computers suffocate blend into some larger whole that reorients the mind, that offers a reward greater than any posted by pure physical exercise. Discovery is not elementary perhaps, but rarely impossible, rarely especially difficult. Exploration is second nature, a second nature intimately linked to the adolescent days of tattered sneakers and old Raleighs, a second nature lost in these turn-of-the-millennium days, but a second nature easy enough to recover any weekday evening, any Sunday morning, any hour snatched away from programmed learning, from the webs and nets that invisibly and insidiously snare.

Physical exercise alone never quite succeeds.

Pretending to walk or ski on some throbbing, conveyor-belt machine or bicycling an Exercycle aligned in front of the television dismays and defeats for good reason. A person is more than separated mind and body, and the body exists as much to carry the mind as the mind exists to direct the body. Outdoors, away from things experts have already explained, the slightly thoughtful person willing to look around carefully for a few minutes, to scrutinize things about which he or she knows nothing in particular, begins to be aware, to notice, to explore. And almost always, that person starts to understand, to see great cultural and social and economic and political patterns unnoticed by journalists and other experts. In that understanding may come a desire to *cry out,* to tell friends or family or total strangers about discoveries great and small, but the understanding may just as well produce a secrecy, a quiet smile, a satisfied nod. Whatever else that understanding of exploration, of discovery, brings, it brings a specialness, a near magic to the explorer that attracts other people who want to know what is so worth looking at.

And maybe exploring ordinary landscape shakes, then shatters the walls that direct the thinking of so many Americans now, both children and adults, the victims of advertising and television and computer networks and scheduled school and work. Risking the shattering of those walls is worth all the risks of going for a long, careful walk, for riding a bicycle down a different street, for seeing what no one photographs, for noticing what no one realizes.

Whoever owns the real estate and its constituents, the explorer owns the landscape.

And the explorer owns all the insights, all the magic that comes from looking.